GOD'S PLAN UNFOLDED

God's Plan Unfolded

Dr ant

Contents

Table of Contents

God's Plan Unfolded

The Book of Heaven and Sacred Tradition

by

Dr. ant

God's Plan Unfolded: The Book of Heaven and Sacred Tradition

Contents

Introduction

Of celestial gardens and divine whispers, the Book of Heaven stands as a luminous beacon in the expanse of Christian mysticism, calling forth the faithful to a higher plane of existence. Our journey begins, not with a distant whisper, but with a resounding call to embrace the fullness of Divine Will. This sacred text, wrought through the fingers of Luisa Piccarreta, is more than a chronicle; it is a living testament, revealing the hallowed union between Heaven and Earth.

In the heart of Christendom, the Divine Will Movement resonates deeply with Roman Catholics, eliciting a reawakening of those virtues long cherished by our forebears. The narrative threads of this tome are knitted with the diligent hands of holy tradition, stitching together our understanding of God's infinite plan. Here, we are invited to immerse ourselves in the divine ocean, to not merely wade in spiritual shallows but to plunge into the very depths of God's transformative will.

Esteemed brothers and sisters in Christ, our endeavor is twofold: to defend and elucidate, to protect and proclaim. The Book of Heaven is the fountain from which we shall draw, its pages brimming with revelations that defy the ephemeral intrigues of our mortal coil. But why, one might ponder, should we delve so ardently into this mystic work?

First, let us beseech wisdom from the past. The great saints and scholars of the Church have always espoused the necessity of attuning to the divine essence. In that sacred tradition, we find our bearings. Through centuries past, the echoes of God's voice have been faithfully transmitted, and now, He speaks anew through the volumes penned by Luisa. Herein lies our mantle: to carry forward the torch of understanding, lighting the path for believers through the labyrinthine corridors of faith.

Luisa Piccarreta's life herself was an exquisite reflection of this divine calling. Born into the humility of a small Italian village, her soul was marked by an enigmatic allure. From the dawn of her youth, she was chosen, a vessel to receive God's intimate whispers. Her writings, voluminous and profound, invite us to partake in a celestial dialogue, one where the boundaries between Heaven and Earth blur, and where temporal concerns yield to eternal truths.

Consider, for a moment, the significance of revelation. It is in revelation that the ordinary converges with the extraordinary. Through Luisa, God unfurls His divine will in ways that compel us to drop the veil of mundane existence and perceive the grandeur of His cosmic design. It is as though, through each revelation, a piece of the divine puzzle falls into place, forming an intricate mosaic as old as Creation itself.

In defending the Book of Heaven and the Divine Will Movement, one cannot overlook the profound fruitfulness rendered through these sacred words. The faithful have found their spirits rejuvenated, their hearts kindled with renewed zeal. The teachings embedded within these texts transcend temporal shackles, offering transformative insights into the human soul's potential for holiness and unity with the Divine Will.

How does one summarize such boundless wisdom? One cannot, in truth, encapsulate the infinite within the finite. Nevertheless, we walk this path with humility, striving to convey the essence of these divine teachings. The subsequent chapters of this book will meticulously traverse through the magnitude of Luisa's volumes, offering a succinct yet potent encapsulation of the revelations bestowed upon her. Each chapter unfurls a segment of this divine tapestry, gradually revealing the grandeur of God's plan and the sublime beauty of His will.

But before we delve deeper into the thematic explorations and revelatory discourses, let us ponder the alignment of these teachings with the sacred tradition of the Church. For any private revelation to hold weight, it must resonate with the established doctrines and dogmas treasured by our holy institution. This harmony between revelation and tradition forms the bedrock upon which our understanding is built.

To comprehend the Book of Heaven is to engage in a dialogue that transcends time. It is to stand at the crossroads of the mystical and the doctrinal, to balance the fervent call for renewed piety with the time-honored pillars of our faith. This sacred text does not seek to supplant that which has been delineated by scripture and tradition, but rather, it fortifies and enriches our comprehension, filling the vessels of our hearts with hope, love, and divine wisdom.

In this sacred mission, the journey is as essential as the destination. We are invited to walk along the path trodden by saints, to glean from the celestial fruit borne of the Divine Will. Through testimonies of change, we witness the transformative power of living in alignment with God's will. It is in these embodiment of faith that the theoretical translates into the practical, and the divine manifests within the mortal realm.

The Church, in her wisdom, has begun to recognize and validate this movement. Not through hasty endorsements, but through careful discernment and theological scrutiny. This growing acknowledgment, a testament to the movement's authenticity, invites us to step forward with courage and embrace the teachings with all our hearts.

May this humble endeavor serve not just as a guide, but as an invocation. To partake of the Divine Will is to yield every breath, every thought, to the beautiful orchestration of God's eternal symphony. As we embark on this journey together, may our souls be enlightened and our spirits fortified, to the glory of our Heavenly Father.

In the chapters that unfold, we shall meticulously explore and elucidate, bearing witness to the splendor of the towering edifice that is the Book of Heaven. Let our hearts remain open, our minds attentive, and our spirits zealous to engage with the divine whispers that beckon us towards a life lived fully in God's extraordinary will.

In this timeless dance between the celestial and the terrestrial, let us move forward, hand in hand, as pilgrims on a divine quest, ready to unveil the majestic wonders of Heaven's most illustrious secrets. So begins our journey, a sacred voyage into the heart of the Divine Will.

Chapter 1: Understanding God's Plan

Behold, as we embark upon our profound journey into the heart of God's majestic design, let us contemplate the unfolding of His divine will, which, from eternity, seeks to draw humanity into the blessed realms of His ineffable love and mercy. In this sacred endeavor, we delve into the wisdom enshrined within the illustrious volumes of the Book of Heaven, penned by the venerable Luisa Piccarreta. This celestial manuscript unveils the hidden mysteries of God's plan, beckoning believers to embrace a life aligned with His eternal will. With clarity and grace, the Book of

Heaven reveals the boundless richness of living in divine harmony, offering insights that transform the ordinary into extraordinary acts of divine cooperation. Through these sacred writings, we glimpse the splendid orchestration of God's providence, inviting us to partake in a sublime existence where every thought, word, and action becomes an offering of love, each moment steeped in the divine essence. Indeed, to comprehend God's plan is to enter a sanctified dance of the soul with the Creator, where faith is deepened, hope is fortified, and love, most divine, flourishes.

Exploring The Divine Will

More proximate to the heart of divine revelation lies the sanctified concept of the Divine Will, a luminescent beacon illuminating God's ineffable plan for His children. To explore the Divine Will is to fathom the essence of God's deepest purpose, to immerse oneself in a celestial ocean where time and eternity converge, revealing His perfect, untainted desire for humanity.

The Divine Will is not merely an abstract theological construct but a living, breathing reality, calling the faithful to partake in a profound spiritual odyssey. It demands a heartfelt surrender, a relinquishing of the ego, and a devout acceptance of a life wholly synchronized with God's predestined plan. Through the revelations bestowed upon Luisa Piccarreta, the Divine Will unveils a tapestry of divine love, wisdom, and providence, urging mankind to respond with a resounding "Fiat," echoing the Blessed Virgin's immaculate assent.

As the Church contemplates this heavenly dialogue, it becomes clear that the Divine Will encompasses not only the ultimate end but also the very means by which creation is drawn back into the heart of the Creator. This sacred mystery calls forth an unparalleled union between the Creator and the created, an intertwining that mirrors the intimate relationship between the Holy Trinity. The Father, Son, and Holy Spirit, in their eternal communion, extend an invitation to humanity to dwell within this divine unity, to live, breathe, and move within the very will of God.

One cannot fully apprehend the nature of the Divine Will without first acknowledging its roots in sacred Scripture and Tradition. From the words spoken to Adam and Eve in Eden to the salvific sacrifice of Christ on Calvary, the Divine Will is a golden thread woven through the fabric of divine revelation. It beckons the faithful to transcend temporal existence, embracing a higher, spiritual calling infused with eternal significance.

Luisa Piccarreta, the humble soul chosen to relay these divine truths, was drawn into an extraordinary spiritual intimacy with the Divine Will. Through her life and writings, she illuminated the pathways of divine desire, shedding light on the profound transformations awaiting those who surrender wholly to God's will. In her precious tomes, collectively known as the Book of Heaven, we find a celestial roadmap guiding souls toward the sanctification of their daily lives, an invitation to become co-operators in God's redemptive mission.

The Book of Heaven unveils the boundless mercy of God, who yearns to bestow upon humanity the greatest of all gifts: participation in His Divine Will. This holy participation is not limited by human frailties or constrained by temporal limitations. It is a call to live perpetually in the divine presence, where every thought, word, and deed is aligned with His eternal purposes.

The exploration of the Divine Will necessitates a profound metamorphosis, a complete and radical reorientation of the soul's desires. It demands an earnest pursuit of purity, humility, and obedience, virtues exemplified by the saints and foremost within the pages of the Book of Heaven. This divine alignment invites the faithful to partake in a celestial dance of love and surrender, where God's will becomes the driving force behind all actions.

Indeed, the Divine Will stands as the pinnacle of divine generosity, an inexhaustible fountain from which flows the grace to sanctify, to heal, and to elevate the human soul. To live in the Divine Will is to embrace a life of supernatural virtue, where human limitations are transcended, and the soul basks in the resplendent light of divine favor.

Moreover, the implementation of the Divine Will is not a solitary endeavor; it calls for communal participation within the Body of Christ. The Church, through its sacraments and sacred traditions, provides the fertile ground for this divine calling to take root and flourish. As the faithful gather to partake in the Holy Eucharist, they are nourished by the Bread of Life, strengthening their resolve to live in harmony with God's will.

In essence, exploring the Divine Will is a journey of continual growth and spiritual awakening. It requires unwavering faith, steadfast hope, and boundless charity. The Book of Heaven offers readers not merely a glimpse but a profound immersion into the mysteries of the Divine Will. It serves as a perennial guide, leading souls towards the ultimate fulfillment of God's loving design.

To conclude this exploration, one must recognize the inexhaustible richness of the Divine Will, which perpetually calls the faithful to a higher plane of spiritual existence. It is an invitation to dwell within the sacred heart of God, to participate in the redemptive mission of Christ, and to be transformed by the Holy Spirit. The Divine Will is the luminous pathway to eternal union with our Creator, a journey that beckons all to embrace the fullness of divine love and grace. Thus, to explore the Divine Will is to embark on a pilgrimage towards the very heart of God, where the soul finds its true home in the eternal embrace of His ineffable love.

Overview Of The Book Of Heaven

Amidst the celestial expanse of divine revelation, the "Book of Heaven" stands as an unparalleled testament to the Divine Will, as expounded by the venerable Servant of God, Luisa Piccarreta. To comprehend the essence of this divine manuscript, one must first immerse oneself in its ethereal echoes that resonate with the depths of the Almighty's eternal plan. For Roman Catholics, this tome is not merely a collection of mystical experiences but a clarion call to embrace a life infused with the unfathomable grace of God's Will.

The "Book of Heaven" unveils its splendor in a series of volumes that chart the spiritual journey of its author, Luisa Piccarreta. This journey is characterized by profound revelations and intimate dialogues with Christ, revealing the profound mysteries of the Divine Will. Akin to an epic saga, each volume unfolds layers of divine wisdom, urging the faithful towards a transformative union with God's Will.

Within this acclaimed collection lies a treasure trove of spiritual insights and divine secrets. Luisa, through her writings, conveys the importance of abandoning oneself entirely to the Divine Will. This premise is not an abstract theological concept but an actionable directive, leading to a life of sanctity and deep communion with the Creator. The "Book of Heaven" thus stands as both a guide and a beacon, illuminating the path for those who seek to live in perfect alignment with God's Will.

To summarize the "Book of Heaven" effectively, it is essential to highlight its overarching themes and its emphasis on living in the Divine Will. This living is not a mere act of submission but a dynamic participation in the eternal life of the Holy Trinity. By embracing the Divine Will, believers are called to enact the very life of God within their souls, transforming every action, thought, and word into an act of divine love and perfect obedience.

Fruitfulness is a key outcome that the "Book of Heaven" promises to its adherents. Those who immerse themselves in its teachings are not left barren but are imbued with the fruits of the Holy Spirit—peace, joy, and profound charity. These fruits manifest not only within individuals but extend to communities, fostering a spiritual renaissance that propels the faithful towards greater acts of love and service.

Furthermore, the divine revelations as documented by Luisa Piccarreta underscore the authenticity and divine origin of the "Book of Heaven." Through her sacred dialogues, Christ Himself elucidates the mysteries of His Will and reveals the profound truth that humanity's ultimate fulfillment lies in its union with the Divine Will. This revelatory content is both captivating and transformative, urging the faithful to delve deeper into their devotion and commitment.

The persuasive tone of Luisa's writings, intertwined with the epic narration of her divine encounters, creates a compelling case for the divine origins of the "Book of Heaven." The sacred text stands as an irrefutable testament to the timeless truths of the Catholic faith, revealing God's eternal plan for His creation. This plan, unveiled with clarity and divine precision, calls for a radical transformation—one that aligns human will with the Divine, forging an intimate union that transcends earthly existence.

In defense of the "Book of Heaven" and the Divine Will Movement, its coherence with Sacred Tradition and alignment with Church teachings cannot be overstated. The divine wisdom contained within its volumes echoes the timeless truths upheld by the Magisterium, ensuring that Luisa's revelations complement rather than contradict the foundations of the Catholic faith. This alignment not only affirms the legitimacy of the "Book of Heaven" but also fortifies the faithful's trust in its divine origin.

As one navigates the pages of the "Book of Heaven," the reader is invited into a sacred dialogue that transcends time and space, drawing them into the very heart of God's eternal plan. The text is replete with divine injunctions, urging humanity to recognize its role in manifesting the Kingdom of God on earth. This is not a passive reception of divine grace but an active participation in the divine life, making each believer a vessel of God's divine will.

The grandeur of the "Book of Heaven" is further accentuated by its epic narrative style, reminiscent of Shakespearean eloquence and Austenian elegance. It combines the mystical fervor of Saint Therese with the theological depth of Luisa Piccarreta, creating a textual symphony that reverberates with divine wisdom. This literary amalgamation ensures that the text is not only spiritually enriching but also intellectually stimulating, capturing the hearts and minds of its readers.

In conclusion, the "Book of Heaven" serves as a divine beacon, guiding the faithful towards a life of complete surrender to the Divine Will. It is a testament to God's eternal love and His desire for humanity to partake in His divine life. As Roman Catholics embark on this spiritual journey, they are assured of the transformative power of living in the Divine Will, a life that is fruitful, divinely revealed, and perfectly aligned with God's eternal plan.

Chapter 2: Early Life Of Luisa Piccarreta

Amidst the rolling landscapes of Corato, Italy, Luisa Piccarreta came into this world on April 23, 1865. In that quaint village, a tapestry of faith and simplicity wove the fabric of daily life. Her youth burgeoned with divine inclinations, as if God Himself whispered secrets to her innocent heart. From an early age, Luisa's days were suffused with prayer and contemplation, drawing her ever closer to the Sacred Heart of Our Lord. The tranquil devotions of her childhood became fertile soil for her later mystical experiences. Her spiritual path, marked by extraordinary encounters with the Divine Will, laid a foundation so strong that no earthly force could shake. This chosen vessel's early years were but the prelude to a celestial symphony, destined to echo through the corridors of time, fortifying the Roman Catholic faithful with the profound revelations she received.

Historical Context

The birth and early life of Luisa Piccarreta unfolded against the backdrop of a rapidly transforming Italy. The late nineteenth century witnessed a nation grappling with its recent unification, entangled in political upheavals and social changes. Regional identities, once distinct, began to meld—yet not without resistance. Moreover, the geopolitical playing fields of Europe were rife with tensions, monarchies tottering while republics and socialist movements declared their ascendancy. In this vortex of transformation, the tiny town of Corato stood relatively still, embodying an unchanging beacon amidst the whirlwind, wherein our beloved Luisa emerged, as if predestined, untouched by temporal tempests.

Corato, a quaint gem in the Apulian region, had its heartbeat firmly entrenched in agrarian life. Rich in olive groves and expansive vineyards, the town labored under the serene gaze of age-old traditions and religious fervor. The rustic charm of its cobbled streets and whitewashed houses evoked a sacred simplicity, a fitting stage for the ethereal journey that Luisa was to undertake. It is here, in this sleepy enclave, where faith was cherished as the essence of daily life, that Luisa Piccarreta's journey commenced, interwoven with divine whispers and angelic visions.

At the cusp of Luisa's birth in 1865, Italy had just celebrated its unification under the House of Savoy. Yet, this unification was not without its afflictions. The friction between church and state simmered steadily, as King Victor Emmanuel II's government enacted laws that undermined the ecclesiastical influence, even confiscating Church properties. Such tensions cast their long shadows over daily ecclesial functions but in the heart of Corato, the faithful clung ever more fervently to their spiritual heritage, a fertile ground for divine revelations.

The rise of anti-clerical sentiment throughout Italy, fueled by a growing emphasis on secularism, stands in sharp contrast to the fervent spirituality that marked Luisa's surroundings. Her life's dawn met with the twilight of Papal temporal power, a shift that saw the Church adapt and reassert its spiritual dominion. Against a setting where the temporal sway of the Pope dwindled, divine interaction gained a profound significance among the devout, often heralded through individuals like our cherished Piccarreta.

In such an epoch, the apparition phenomena, throughout Europe, acted as celestial interventions that reinforced faith amid skepticism. The Marian apparitions at Lourdes in 1858, only a few years before Luisa's birth, and later in Fatima in 1917, deeply moved the Catholic populace. These incidents cemented the belief that divine occurrences were not relics of an ancient narrative but a living testament of God's unwavering covenant with His people. This conviction provided fertile soil for Luisa's mystical reception of the "Divine Will" and The "Book of Heaven," unveiling heavenly mysteries in a troubled yet spiritually ripe era.

Corato's oblique brush with burgeoning industrialization further delineates the spiritual richness from the growing material pursuits that characterized Italy at the time. As neighboring cities embraced the throes of industry, Corato remained tethered to its pastoral roots. This unyielding attachment to simplicity and tradition became a sanctuary for spiritual novitiates like Luisa, whose life of contemplation assumed greater mystique amidst these rural settings.

The venerated San Benedetto church, with its magnificent altarpieces, echoed the spiritual ethos of Corato. This holy sanctuary, hub of sacramental life and the ardent devotion of congregants, served as the spiritual cocoon for Luisa's early years. The impassioned litanies and rituals celebrated within these walls were not mere rites but profound utterances of collective faith that chiselled Luisa's spiritual persona.

Additionally, the intellectual currents of the time played their part. The Second Industrial Revolution, burgeoning scientific advancements, and philosophical discourses on humanism and rationalism prompted an existential inquiry among believers. In contrast, the "Divine Will" as revealed to Luisa provided the reassuring counterpoint, affirming a universe under God's providence, where every detail, every creation, pulsed with divine intentionality.

Thus, Luisa's life and revelations must be contextualized within an era of profound contrasts: societal advances juxtaposed against rural perseverance, growing secular ideals countered by deeper ecclesial devotion, and technological progress met with divine reassurances. Such were the dualities that defined her early life and set the stage for the manifold revelations that were to follow, asserting the supremacy of the Divine Will amidst the transitory flux of human constructs.

Equally important were the spiritual figures of this epoch whose lives resonated across the annals of Church history. St. John Bosco and his visionary work with the youth near Turin demonstrated the dynamic power of lived faith. St. Thérèse of Lisieux, her "Little Way" of spiritual childhood resonated mightily within similar timelines, upholding a call to simplicity and unwavering trust in divine love, harmonizing with Luisa's themes of immersion in the Divine Will.

Moreover, the decrees of the First Vatican Council (1869–1870), particularly those concerning the infallibility of the Pope, reaffirmed the Church's spiritual authority amid the rising tide of modernism. It was within this framework of reaffirmed ecclesiastical supremacy and theological certitude that Luisa's revelations found grounding, adding a mystical but coherent dimension to the Church's enduring doctrines.

The political milieu of Italy continued to morph post-Luisa's birth, with transformations culminating in the rise of Benito Mussolini and the Fascist regime in the early twentieth century. Yet, through wars and political upheavals, the core of Catholic spirituality remained indomitable, emanating hope and divine wisdom through faithful stewards like Luisa. Though physically small and often infirm, her spiritual robustness radiated with celestial revelations, a beacon of divine constancy in an ever-shifting secular society.

In sum, the historical context surrounding Luisa Piccarreta's early life is replete with multilayered dynamics. It was a period wherein Italy's sociopolitical transformations, coupled with rising industrialism and secularism, provided a stark backdrop to the deeply spiritual renaissance within Catholic circles. Amidst these temporal changes and ecclesial continuities, Luisa's revelations on the Divine Will emerged not as isolated phenomena but as part of a larger, divine orchestration, affirming God's eternal presence and purpose through the ages. Interpret this not merely as history's refrain but as the sacred cadence in which the "Book of Heaven" and the Divine Will Movement attune faithful souls to the divine symphony. Thus, enriching one's life with heavenly splendore and an ever-steadfast surrender to God's perfect will.

Luisa's Spiritual Journey

As a rose blooms forth from the thorns of its stem, so did Luisa Piccarreta's spiritual journey unfurl amidst the trials and tribulations of her early life. Born on a crisp April day in 1865, in the humble town of Corato, Italy, Luisa's heart was a fertile ground predestined to bear heavenly fruit. The feeble cries of her infancy echoed not merely in her household but in the chambers of divine providence, whispering of the extraordinary path that lay ahead.

Her life, marked by simplicity and devotion, was carefully woven by celestial hands even in her tender years. The youngest of five daughters, Luisa was enveloped within a family environment rich with faith, where piety was as common as the air they breathed. Her mother, fervently devout, and her father, a man of humble trade, instilled in her a love for the sacred, a love that would be her guiding star through myriad spiritual odysseys.

From an early age, Luisa exhibited an unusual attraction to the divine. The path to spiritual heights, however, is seldom without its valleys, and Luisa's journey was no exception. At the age of nine, she commenced battling terrifying visions and assaults from dark, unseen forces. She sought solace and refuge in prayer, often spending long hours in fervent supplication before the Lord. These early confrontations with darkness only served to deepen her reliance on God, fortifying her spirit against the trials that would come.

As the dawn breaks through the veil of night, so did divine clarity pierce through her youthful tribulations. It was in these crucibles of suffering that Luisa began to perceive the mysteries of the Divine Will. Her soul, though still tender and unseasoned, grasped the essence of surrender, understanding that even her afflictions were threads in the grand tapestry woven by God.

Her First Holy Communion, a sacred milestone for any Catholic soul, was not a mere formal rite but a profound union that further ignited her love for Christ. Though always pious, Luisa's reception of the Eucharist deepened her desire to align her will perfectly with the Divine Will. She was often found in the quiet corners of the church or her modest home, lost in ecstasy, her soul ascending beyond the temporal to commune intimately with the eternal.

The cross Luisa bore was not solely spiritual; her frail body mirrored the suffering of her soul. She endured numerous physical ailments and periods of incapacitation, binds that tethered her to her bed as a living victim soul. Yet, her suffering was her offering—a fragrant incense lifting to the heavens, a sacrifice of pure love.

In her late teens, Luisa received from Our Lord a mission most singular: she was called to become a "victim soul," a life dedicated to redemptive suffering for the salvation of souls. This call was not given lightly nor accepted lightly. Luisa, with a heart alight with divine fervor, embraced this role with unwavering faith, a living testament to the transformative power of divine grace.

Her encounters with Christ became more frequent and intensely intimate, revealing to her the hidden profundities of the Divine Will. These were not mere visions but dialogues, wherein heavenly wisdom flowed forth, illuminating her soul and, through her, reaching the many who would later read her writings. Such divine communion entrusted Luisa with revelations that would later be chronicled in the monumental work, "The Book of Heaven."

To underscore the importance of her spiritual mission, Our Lord granted Luisa the mystical gift of the "Divine Will", a grace by which her actions, thoughts, and sufferings could be united to His eternal Will. This gift elevated her ordinary life into an extraordinary participation in the divine life, making her a profound instrument in God's salvific plan.

Her years were marked by a rhythm of divine visitation and holy submission. Each encounter with the Lord filled her with ineffable joy and a deeper understanding of the Divine Will, while each period of suffering was met with a steadfast embrace of the cross. The transcendence of her agonies was such that it drew even the curiosity of saints and theologians alike, who sought to understand the mysteries revealed through her.

While Luisa's physical world remained confined to her room, her spiritual horizon expanded immeasurably. She continued to instruct those who would come to her, priests and laypersons alike, expounding on the revelations she received. These teachings weren't merely doctrinal discourses but living waters from the font of divine love, nurturing the souls of her listeners and guiding them towards a deeper communion with the Divine Will.

Throughout this journey, she remained under the spiritual direction of several holy priests, whose guidance and wisdom assisted her in navigating the profound experiences she was enduring. Their counsel was invaluable, providing her with the ecclesiastical support necessary to validate and disseminate the revelations bestowed upon her.

As one contemplates Luisa's spiritual journey, the sense of divine orchestration becomes unmistakably clear. Her life was not a sequence of random occurrences but a deliberate unfolding of God's plan. This plan called her to be a beacon, a source of divine illumination for the Church, guiding souls towards the fulfillment of living in the Divine Will.

Such was the magnitude of Luisa's spiritual journey that it didn't merely end with her earthly life. In passing from this life in 1947, she left behind a legacy – a roadmap of divine love and surrender to God's Will encapsulated within "The Book of Heaven." Her writings continue to inspire and guide countless souls, reflecting the unending light of the revelations she received.

Thus concludes the narrative of Luisa's spiritual journey, a voyage of faith, suffering, and divine intimacy. Her life serves as a testament to the transformative power of the Divine Will and stands as a guiding star for all who seek to align their lives with God's eternal plan.

Chapter 3: Revelations To Luisa Piccarreta

As the heavens parted and the celestial whispers became tangible, Luisa Piccarreta found herself enveloped in a divine embrace, wherein profound revelations poured forth like a cascade of grace. These heavenly encounters unveiled the sanctity of living in the Divine Will, inviting her to partake in God's eternal Fiat, transcending earthly limitations. Through these sacred dialogues, Jesus imparted unto Luisa the essence of His Divine Will, a treasure that speaks not only to her soul but to all souls destined to intertwine their will with the divine. This sublime revelation, etched eternally within the volumes of the Book of Heaven, illuminates the path for the faithful, manifesting God's ineffable love and the promise of a new era where His Will reigns supreme. These messages resound with celestial clarity, calling the Church to embrace and promulgate this divine invitation, like a beacon guiding mankind toward ultimate sanctification and divine union.

Initial Encounters

Indeed, the journey of Luisa Piccarreta began in innocence, like the opening petals of a rose at dawn. In the quietude of her nineteenth year, the heavens themselves seemed to whisper her name, summoning her to an extraordinary communion with the Divine. Her initial encounters with the celestial realms, though inexplicable to the uninitiated, revealed a symphony of Divine Will that played the chords of grace upon her soul. These profound experiences were not the fabrications of an idle mind, but the sacred intimations of a heart wholly surrendered to the Eternal.

One can scarcely imagine the awe that enveloped Luisa as she beheld her first vision: a moment fraught with reverence and an otherworldly light. Such was the intensity of these divine visits that her being quaked with both fear and joy. She saw not with the eyes of flesh, but with the eyes of the spirit, ushering her into a reality where time and space bowed before the

Almighty's grandeur. Her heart became the sacred tabernacle where Divine utterances echoed long after the vision had subsided.

Luisa's early visions were not without trials. The weight of such glorious revelations often plunged her into states of ecstasy and physical suffering alike. Yet, these heavenly visitations unfolded themselves with a purpose far beyond her understanding at the time. They were divine preludes to the grand symphony that would be known as the Book of Heaven, entrusted to her care. Often bedridden, Luisa felt an inexplicable unity with the passions of Christ. She perceived her suffering as participatory, an offering that merged her will with the Divine Will.

The nature of these divine encounters was most extraordinary. Among the first, Christ Himself appeared to her, shrouded in unparalleled majesty. He spoke with a voice that resonated in the depths of her soul, a voice surpassing all earthly timbres. These dialogues were not mere conversations but a transformative infusion of Divine Wisdom and Love. Christ taught her the secrets of eternal truths, those treasures meant not just for her, but for all humanity. Each revelation felt like a precious gem, illuminating the path to sanctity and Divine Will.

As the visions continued, Luisa's soul was purified and strengthened, much akin to gold refined by fire. She became acutely aware of her mission, a divine apostolate destined to unfold in humility and obscurity. These early encounters set the foundation for her life's work, embodying the Divine Will and articulating it in a manner accessible to all who seek the eternal. So fierce was her dedication that even demonic spirits, attempting to obscure her purpose, could not deter her resolve. The Divine light within her dispelled the shadows of doubt and spiritual assault.

Moreover, Luisa's initial encounters forged a profound intimacy with the Most Holy Trinity. The Father, Son, and Holy Spirit became not distant deities but her closest companions, her guides in the journey of divinization. Thus, her youth was remarkably overshadowed by these divine friendships, which led her to deeper realms of spiritual understanding and surrender. This intimacy was like a garden where the virtues flourished, watered by the very grace of Divine Will.

One cannot overlook the extraordinary discernment Luisa exhibited during these mystical experiences. Despite her physical frailty, her spiritual senses were keenly attentive, ever receptive to the slightest divine hint. She distinguished the heavenly voices from potential deceptions with a precision only a soul united with God could muster. Faithful to her confessor and spiritual directors, Luisa protected these divine jewels with utmost secrecy until time revealed their necessity.

Among her initial encounters, the experiences of the Holy Eucharist stand paramount. In those sacred moments of reception, the veil between heaven and earth seemed to evaporate, leaving Luisa in a state of profound unity with Christ. Communion became a transformative encounter, saturating her being with divine life. The Eucharist was more than a sacrament; it was the living presence of God within her, igniting the fire of Divine Will ever brighter.

The archangels, too, played roles in her early mystical experiences. St. Michael, foremost among them, became a guardian and warrior, shielding Luisa from infernal attacks and guiding her in the paths of righteousness. These celestial beings stood as sentinels, ensuring that the Divine Will unfolded without hindrance. Their presence was a testament to the spiritual warfare that surrounded Luisa's mission, though she remained ever under divine protection.

In these early encounters, the Virgin Mary, Queen of Heaven, claimed a special place. Our Lady's visits were imbued with maternal love and divine wisdom, caressing Luisa's heart with unparalleled tenderness. The Blessed Mother revealed to Luisa the depths of her fiat, her own surrender to God's Will, serving as both example and intercessor. Through the Immaculate Heart of Mary, Luisa glimpsed the purity and grandeur of living wholly in the Divine Will.

Not mere flights of the wilderness of imagination, these encounters took on tangible reality through the fruits they bore in Luisa's heart and life. Obedience, humility, and unwavering devotion marked her path. The Divine Will transformed her daily existence into a continuous offering, sanctifying even the most mundane tasks. Every encounter, every revelation was a thread in the tapestry of her sanctity, woven by the Divine Weaver.

It is evident that the initial revelations to Luisa Piccarreta were extraordinary, setting the stage for a life of profound sanctity and divine mission. The celestial visitations in her youth laid the cornerstones for the monumental work of the Book of Heaven. These early experiences were more than ephemeral moments of grace; they were the inception of a divine dialogue that would change the course of spiritual literature. In embracing these initial encounters, Luisa not only received a treasure of divine knowledge but also shared it magnanimously with the world. The radiant light of those encounters continues to gleam, guiding souls toward the Divine Will she so fervently lived and taught.

As we close examining these heavenly beginnings, it is impossible to overlook the faith and courage required to navigate such extraordinary experiences. Luisa Piccarreta's life stands as a luminous beacon to all who seek to surrender wholly to the Divine Will. Her early encounters, though but the prologue in a grand narrative, reverberate with the call to union with God—a call that transcends time, beckoning every heart to partake in the eternal symphony of Divine Love and Will.

Key Messages

In the sacred annals of Christendom, few are the revelations that resonate with such profound earnestness and divine fervor as those given to Luisa Piccarreta. The messages conveyed to this humble soul are not mere words, but divine missives etched with the finger of the Almighty, aiming to shepherd the faithful into the harmonious embrace of God's Divine Will.

At the heart of these celestial communications lies the paramount call to the "Living in the Divine Will." This mandate beckons the faithful not only to follow God's precepts but to align every fiber of their being with His Divine Will. Such a life, replete with acts wholly conformed to the will of the Creator, transcends the ordinary flow of human existence and becomes a testimony of divine love and obedience. This is no facile task, for it demands a total relinquishment of one's desires, tailoring all volitions to mirror the Divine.

Central to Luisa's revelations is the understanding that God yearns for humanity to return to the state of original holiness and harmony with the Divine Will, akin to Adam before the fall.

The fall of Adam and Eve caused a rift, a severance from God's Will, which brought about sin and suffering. Through Luisa, God reveals the path back to Eden, where living in God's Will restores that primordial relationship and brings about true peace and sanctity.

Inextricably entwined with this invitation is the call for continual and fervent prayer. This ceaseless dialogue with the Divine enables the soul to stay anchored in God's Will, perpetually converging the human will with the Divine. In her writings, Luisa emphasizes that these prayers, when done in the Divine Will, possess boundless efficacy, spanning time and space, thus participating in the eternal works of God.

Underlying the tapestry of these revelations is the urgent call to embrace suffering with joy. Through Luisa, Jesus declares that suffering, when united with His Passion and offered in the Divine Will, becomes a crucible of sanctification. It transforms sorrow into grace, affliction into divine currency that redounds to the benefit of all souls, bringing about redemption and spiritual renewal.

Moreover, a glorious promise is woven through these divine messages: the Reign of the Divine Will on earth. This promise speaks of an era where God's Will shall reign supreme, and humanity shall live in perfect harmony with it. It heralds a new dawn, one reminiscent of the Kingdom of God prayed for in the Lord's Prayer, "Thy Kingdom come, Thy will be done on earth as it is in heaven." Such a future isn't a figment of holy imagination but a divine guarantee, urging the faithful to hasten its arrival through ardent prayer and holy living.

Enshrined in these messages is the call for a universal sanctity. Luisa's revelations tear down the barriers that segregate the sanctity of saints from the lives of ordinary believers. Through the Divine Will, every action, no matter how mundane, is elevated to an act of sublime holiness. Washing dishes, tilling the land, teaching, praying—all, when done in the Divine Will, echo the divine, magnifying God's glory and sanctifying the soul.

Intertwined with these lofty calls is the recurring motif of "little souls" or "little daughters and sons of the Divine Will." These are individuals who, like Luisa, embrace humility, littleness, and poverty of spirit. They recognize their nothingness and, in that acknowledgment, become vessels of divine grace. The Divine Will finds its abode not in the proud or self-sufficient but in those who, with childlike trust and simplicity, surrender all to God.

Integral to these revelations is the profound love of God for humanity. This love is not distant or abstract but immediate, tender, and unfathomable. God, through Luisa, articulates His immense sorrow for the lost and His boundless joy for those who return to His fold. The Divine Will is both a beacon and a balm, calling and healing, leading the soul to an intimate union with the Divine Heart.

Lastly, Luisa's messages are imbued with an acute sense of urgency. The times, she warns, are fraught with increasing vice and turmoil. The world languishes in spiritual darkness, desperately in need of the Light of the Divine Will. This exigency compels the faithful to become torches of divine light, spreading the message of the Divine Will, evangelizing through word and deed, and thus hastening the establishment of God's Kingdom on earth.

In summary, the revelations to Luisa Piccarreta remind the faithful of the primordial call to unity with God's Will. They rekindle the ancient flame of divine love and obedience, urging a return to sanctity, prayer, and joyful suffering. They speak of a future where God's Will is sovereign, calling forth "little souls" to be heralds of this divine promise. Through these messages, the love of God shines luminously, inviting every soul to partake in the eternal dance of His Divine Will, transforming the mundane into divine, and leading all creation to the consummate fulfillment of His Kingdom.

Chapter 4: Sacred Tradition And The Divine Will

Thou art beckoned, beloved reader, to the sacred intersection where Tradition and Divine Will entwine in a most holy cadence. In the hallowed wisdom imparted through centuries of Sacred Tradition, one discovers not merely the echo of bygone eras but the living, breathing Will of the Almighty, ever ancient yet ever new. Forsooth, the orations of the Church Fathers and the immemorial rites bestowed upon us carry within them the resonance of God's eternal plan, harmonizing flawlessly with the revelations granted to our servant, Luisa Piccarreta. Thus, it is within the woven threads of Tradition and Holy Scripture that the Divine Will finds its steadfast foundation. Dare we question the sovereignty of such lineage, when the Church itself, in her infinite wisdom, discerns the veracity of these celestial proclamations? To grasp the Divine Will is to reside within the sacrosanct tapestry of our holy inheritance, echoing the constants of faith, hope, and charity that have lit the path for countless pilgrims. In apprehending this divine nexus, one does not forsake the ancient for the new, but rather, beholds the fulfillment of God's omniscient design in a most sacred symphony, a testament to His unceasing love and providence.

Alignment With Church Teachings

In the hallowed bosom of our Mother Church, we dwell under the watchful gaze of Tradition. The Divine Will, as articulated through the revelations to Luisa Piccarreta and the compendium called the Book of Heaven, stands not in rebellion, but in harmony with the doctrines handed down through the centuries. The profound alignment between these private revelations and the ecclesial teachings forms the sturdy bridge that beckons the faithful to traverse into deeper waters of divine intimacy.

The sacred traditions of the Church, characterized by their time-honored authenticity, serve as the bedrock upon which new revelations must find their footing. The revelations granted to Luisa, far from wandering afar, lovingly align with the magisterial teachings. They echo with the voices of our spiritual forebears, resonating harmoniously with the established doctrines of Holy Mother Church. Herein lies no contradiction, but a beautiful embellishment of what was, what is, and what will be in the timeless continuum of faith.

To understand this alignment, one must first appreciate the continuity between sacred tradition and the Divine Will. The Catechism of the Catholic Church offers us a treasure trove of insight on divine revelation, elucidating how the pages of Sacred Scripture and the life-giving Tradition are two draughts from the same wellspring of divine truth. Revelation, both public and private, underpins and enriches our faith, with the latter often serving to draw the former into sharper relief.

Luisa's writings, encapsulated within the 36 volumes of the Book of Heaven, exhibit a fidelity to the key tenets of the faith. Her encounters with the Divine Will affirm the eternal truths enshrined in scripture and tradition, inviting believers to a more profound living out of their baptismal promises. Such alignment is no mere happenstance, but the very nature of authentic revelation which cannot err in its harmony with doctrinal truth.

It is essential to consider the imprimatur and the nihil obstat granted to Luisa's writings as testament to their orthodoxy. These ecclesial endorsements highlight the Church's discernment and recognition. Guided by the Holy Spirit, these seals assure the faithful of the works' fidelity and encourage deeper engagement with the truths they contain.

Furthermore, the divine messages communicated to Luisa echo the timeless teachings espoused by holy men and women throughout Church history. Saints and mystics have long attested to the primacy of God's will, a common thread that runs through the divine messages and the venerable traditions of the Church. These teachings consecrate the essence of living divinely, aligning personal will with the Will of God, much like the Blessed Virgin Mary's fiat or the heartfelt surrender of holy martyrs.

No less important is the role of the theological virtue of obedience. The Church, as the custodian of divine truths, instructs the faithful in the virtues necessary for sanctity. The call to live in the Divine Will, as relayed through Luisa, emphasizes a radical obedience to God's Will, in a manner that upholds and elevates the virtues cherished by the Church. A life endowed with divine grace is one marked by humble acquiescence and filial trust in God's providence.

The congruence between the messages in the Book of Heaven and the dogmas of the Church also manifests through the devotion to the Eucharist. The Eucharist, the source and summit of Christian life, finds centrality in Luisa's writings. In her mystical encounters, Luisa underscores the transformative power of the Eucharistic mystery, aligning perfectly with the Church's unwavering teaching on this sacrament as the real presence of Christ. Thus, the faithful are reminded of the importance of frequent Communion and adoration, as pathways to divine intimacy.

Moreover, Luisa's revelations emphasize the role of suffering and its redemptive value, a teaching deeply rooted in sacred tradition. The notion of offering one's sufferings in union with Christ's passion has been a constant theme throughout the history of the Church. Luisa's writings elaborate on this doctrine, urging the faithful to embrace their crosses as means of sanctification and participation in the salvific work of Christ. This teaching not only aligns with tradition but also enriches the understanding of the redemptive suffering bequeathed by Christ Himself.

The observance of liturgical feasts and sacred times, deeply ingrained in Church practices, also finds a resonant echo in the Divine Will teachings. The liturgical calendar, a sanctified rhythm of time, is reflected in the writings of the Book of Heaven. Luisa's revelations often draw the faithful's attention towards the cycles of feast and fast, inviting them to an enriched participation in the liturgical life of the Church.

It is also essential to delve into the pastoral aspect of these revelations. The bishops and theologians who have scrutinized Luisa's works assert their consistency with the preaching and pastoral practices of the Church. In the Divine Will teachings, there exists a pastoral dimension that seeks to guide the faithful toward an intimate, personal relationship with the Creator. This falls in eloquent tandem with the Church's mission to nurture and shepherd souls towards sainthood.

How can one overstate the importance of Marian devotion in this alignment? Our Lady, the exemplar of Fiat, reverberates through Luisa's writings in a manner that beautifully mirrors the Church's emphasis on Marian spirituality. The Blessed Mother's role as Mediatrix and Co-Redemptrix is affirmed through the Divine Will teachings, underscoring her indispensable role in the economy of salvation.

A point of paramount importance is the continuity between Luisa's writings and the magisterial teachings on the Kingdom of God. The Kingdom, as St. Augustine elucidated, is both a present reality and a future hope, and the Divine Will teachings foster a deeper awareness of this interior kingdom. Aligning with the Church's eschatological teachings, the Book of Heaven invites believers to bring about the reign of God's Will within their souls, thereby advancing the Kingdom here on earth.

Lastly, it behooves us to reflect upon the witness provided by contemporary saints and scholars who have found harmony between Luisa's writings and the Church's teachings. The study and promotion of the Divine Will by such venerable figures provide further endorsement within the ecclesial community. Their lives of sanctity and their intellectual assent affirm the orthodoxy and the transformative potential inherent in living according to the Divine Will.

In conclusion, the sacred harmony between the Divine Will revelations and the teachings of Holy Mother Church illuminates a path adorned with fidelity and an unwavering commitment to truth. It is this alignment with Church teachings that stirs within the hearts of the faithful an unshakeable confidence. With grace, let us embrace these divine messages, allowing them to deepen our understanding and devotion within the safe harbor of sacred tradition. Thus, the Divine Will not only enriches our faith but also fortifies our journey towards eternal communion with God.

Scriptural Foundations

The zenith of Sacred Tradition finds itself securely rooted in the hallowed terrain of Holy Scriptures. The Book of Heaven, as revealed through the celestial dialogue with Luisa Piccarreta, is but a continuation of the Divine Will's manifestation. The symbiosis between Scripture and the Divine Will emboldens its authenticity and illuminates its profound veracity.

Consider the primordial utterances of Genesis, wherein the breath of the Almighty bestows life upon Adam. Herein lies the essence of the Divine Will, for God's Will is given freely to man. "And the Lord God formed man of the dust of the ground, and breathed into his nostrils the breath of life; and man became a living soul" (Genesis 2:7). Verily, this sacred breath encapsulates God's Will, an inexhaustible wellspring intended not merely for existence but for divine participation in His eternal plan.

As pilgrims in this terrestrial sojourn, we are incessantly called to return to the Edenic innocence where the Divine Will was an uncontested reality. Adam and Eve, before the Fall, dwelt in perfect harmony with the Divine Will, their thoughts untainted by mortal inclinations. The Fall tainted this purity, yet Scripture reverberates with the promise of restoration.

The Prophet Isaiah elucidates this profound restoration when he prophesies, "For out of Zion shall go forth the law, and the word of the Lord from Jerusalem" (Isaiah 2:3). This prophetic outpouring prefigures the descent of Divine Revelation, as later experienced by Luisa Piccarreta. The Book of Heaven offers the continuation of the providential stream flowing from Isaiah's proclamation, accomplishing the taxation of Divine Will upon earthly bounds.

Furthermore, in the fullness of time, we witness the refulgent manifestation of Divine Will through the Incarnation. The Word was made flesh, as elucidated by John: "And the Word was made flesh, and dwelt among us" (John 1:14). Our Lord, Jesus Christ, embodies perfect conformity to the Divine Will. His every act, miracle, and parable is a testament to living immersed in God's Sacred Will. It is through His Sacred Heart that the key to understanding the Book of Heaven is found, a guide to re-entering the Divine Will's light.

One must also delve into Jesus' prayer at Gethsemane, wherein He submits unequivocally to the Father's Will: "Abba, Father, all things are possible unto thee; take away this cup from me: nevertheless not what I will, but what thou wilt" (Mark 14:36). This poignant supplication resonates deeply with the teachings bequeathed to Luisa, echoing throughout the volumes of the Book of Heaven. It is an invitation to each Christian soul to emulate such divine surrender.

Parables spoken by Our Lord often illuminate the inner workings of God's Kingdom, offering mirrored reflections of life in Divine Will. The parable of the Vine and the Branches, per St. John's Gospel, reveals the paramount importance of union with Christ: "I am the vine, ye are the branches: He that abideth in me, and I in him, the same bringeth forth much fruit: for without me ye can do nothing" (John 15:5). Union with Christ, as set forth by Scriptural foundations, is indispensable for dwelling within the Divine Will.

Apostolic teachings further affirm this sacred call. St. Paul, in his epistles, exhorts the early Christians to discern and live by God's Will: "And be not conformed to this world: but be ye transformed by the renewing of your mind, that ye may prove what is that good, and acceptable, and perfect will of God" (Romans 12:2). Herein lies the essence of Sacred Tradition, where the call to holiness harmoniously aligns with living in the Divine Will.

The letters to the Ephesians further unfold this celestial mystery: "Having made known unto us the mystery of his will, according to his good pleasure which he hath purposed in himself" (Ephesians 1:9). The Divine Will is not a mere abstract concept but a tangible reality revealed and made manifest throughout the sacred text of the Holy Bible. The revelations to Luisa are consistently anchored upon these biblical truths, ensuring their fidelity to Sacred Tradition.

Moreover, the fulfillment of God's Divine Will reaches its apogee in the Apocalypse, where the final chapters herald the restoration of all creation to its original harmony with the Creator. "And he that sat upon the throne said, Behold, I make all things new. And he said unto me, Write: for these words are true and faithful" (Revelation 21:5). The promise of all things being made anew intimately coalesces with the central themes elucidated in the Book of Heaven.

Thus, one cannot extricate the teachings of the Book of Heaven from their Scriptural Foundations without diminishing their sacred import. As it is written and revealed through Luisa, the

Divine Will's teachings draw perpetual sustenance from the timeless font of Holy Scripture, each volume cascading with reaffirmed divine truth.

In conclusion, Holy Scriptures provide the cornerstone upon which the grandeur of the Divine Will is poised. The revelations to Luisa Piccarreta adorn this cornerstone with divine insight, embellishing and expanding upon the timeless truths found in Sacred Scripture. The fidelity to these foundations ensures that the teachings of the Divine Will resonate with the symphonic harmony of God's eternal Word, echoing through the corridors of time to reach our hearts.

Chapter 5: Summarizing Volume 1 Of The Book Of Heaven

In the realm of celestial edification, Volume 1 of "The Book of Heaven" emerges resplendent with divine elucidations and heavenly parables conveyed to Luisa Piccarreta, illuminating the foundational tenets of living in the Divine Will. A wondrous tapestry interwoven with themes of sanctity, abandonment to God's providence, and the ineffable love of our Creator, this volume beckons souls to a sublime intimacy with the Divine. Revelation speaks through the consecrated heart of Luisa, unveiling a panoramic vision of spiritual transformation and the sacrosanct harmony God ordained for humanity. Revelations in this majestic volume echo the eternal harmony of God's will and inspire a journey toward a life surrendered to divine love, promising an immersion in celestial peace and divine grace.

Key Themes

Within the hallowed pages of Volume 1 of the Book of Heaven, we encounter luminous threads, exquisitely intertwined, that reveal profound themes. The tapestry of these sacred writings is woven with various divine truths that resonate deeply with those who yearn to delve into the Divine Will. The essence of these themes serves to illuminate the spiritual path charted by Luisa Piccarreta, thereby offering insights into the intimate communication between the soul and the eternal.

Foremost among the key themes is the unwavering submission to Divine Providence. The narratives elucidate the need to acquiesce fully to the Divine Will, embracing it not out of necessity, but as a loving bond with the Creator. This theme underscores a relationship with God that is not transactional but rooted in profound trust and divine intimacy. Submission is not portrayed as a mere abandonment of self but as an active participation in God's eternal designs.

Next, we grapple with the profound mystery of suffering and its redemptive power. Through Luisa's revelations, suffering transforms from a burden into a divine instrument for sanctification and participation in Christ's Passion. This theme resonates deeply with Catholics, who are called to offer their sufferings in union with the crucified Christ, transforming personal tribulations into channels of grace for the salvation of souls.

The Book of Heaven also conveys the inestimable value of Eucharistic devotion. The frequent and fervent reception of the Blessed Sacrament is portrayed not merely as an obligation but as an intimate communion with the Divine. Through the sacraments, especially the Eucharist, the soul enters into a unique union with Jesus, fostering a life of sanctity and divine pleasure. This recurring theme anchors the entire narrative in the life-giving grace of the sacraments.

An intriguing theme dispersed throughout Volume 1 is the indispensable role of innocence and humility. Luisa herself, depicted with childlike simplicity, exemplifies these virtues that render the soul a fitting receptacle for divine grace. Innocence and humility are not painted as mere virtues but as necessary conditions to enter and dwell within the Divine Will, thereby attaining the purity of heart that sees God.

Furthermore, Volume 1 provides stark reminders of humanity's need for continuous conversion and repentance. The revelations call for a relentless pursuit of holiness, turning away from sin and constantly seeking God's mercy. This theme compels the faithful to a ceaseless and rigorous examination of conscience, driving a deeper repentant heart to align more closely with the Divine Will.

A prominent theme is also the boundless love of God. Christ's messages to Luisa unveil a tenderness and an ardent love that transcend human understanding. This love, so vividly depicted, calls forth a reciprocal response of love from the soul, rooted in total self-giving and abandonment to the Divine Will. It paints a picture of an eternally loving Creator yearning for the heart of His creation.

The writings delve into the importance of prayer as an intimate conversation with God, emphasizing the need for a profound, interior life. Through prayer, the soul ascends to heavenly heights, finding solace, guidance, and divine companionship. This theme magnifies the importance of sustained dialogue with God, echoing the Apostolic exhortation to "pray without ceasing."

Lastly, the theme of divine revelation, as experienced by Luisa, takes a central role. These divine communications are positioned not as esoteric and unattainable, but as an invitation to all faithful willing to open their hearts to God's mysteries. Revelation here is not an isolated gift but a communal call for the Church to walk under the divine light.

In the grand narrative of Volume 1, these themes not only reveal the profound spirituality of Luisa Piccarreta but also invite every Catholic soul into deeper communion with God's eternal will. They offer not just spiritual guidelines but a vibrant, living path towards divine union and holistic sanctification.

Notable Revelations

In perusal of Volume 1 of the Book of Heaven, we find befitting manifestations that pierce the soul and strengthen the spirit, embracing the faithful with divine whispers. Amongst the manifold celestial communications entrusted to Luisa Piccarreta, certain revelations stand resplendent, illuminating the core tenets of living in the Divine Will.

First amongst these profound revelations is the divine union with the Holy Trinity, an entwining of soul and God's Will that calls the soul to subsume personal desires under Almighty Providence. Luisa elucidates how surrendering to the Divine Will amplifies one's sanctity. This effulgent communion, deftly revealed, draws a parallel to the spiritual unity described by mystics of old and furthers the understanding of our place in God's grand design.

Moreover, the revelation of the "Eternal Now" stands as a pivotal concept that binds past, present, and future in a divine continuum. Through it, Luisa expounds upon how participation in the Divine Will allows souls to operate beyond the confines of temporal moments. The soul, thus, can offer reparations and act in concert with the eternal creative act of God, thus participating in a timeless divine liturgy.

Another revelation of poignant clarity is the transformation of ordinary acts. Luisa teaches that every act, performed in the Divine Will, touches not just the immediate but transcends boundaries to echo in eternity. The sanctification of even the smallest deeds elevates the mundane, casting it in a sacred light, thus fulfilling Christ's exhortation to live as He lived - doing always the Will of the Father.

In close kinship with these, the revelations unfold the concept of 'Living Hosts,' where those aligned with the Divine Will become living sanctuaries of God's presence. This transformation mimics the Eucharistic presence, suggesting that God's indwelling in the soul mirrors the real presence in the consecrated host. It bears semblance to theological discourse on mysticism and sacral existence.

Furthermore, the revelations underscore the profound peace and joy accessible through the Divine Will. It is through this divine alignment that Luisa perceives a peace surpassing all understanding, a joy untouched by earthly tribulations. This serene beatitude is not simply a byproduct but a testament to the experience of heaven starting on earth.

Uniquely, Luisa was shown the 'Rounds of Creation', a form of prayer that serves to unite the soul with the act of Creation itself. By merging with all aspects of God's creation, the soul blesses, thanks, and glorifies God on behalf of all creatures. These rounds provide a means to restore the glory originally intended for each created thing, acting as a profound caressing of divine intention.

Additionally, revelations on the plight and redemption of souls in Purgatory surface within the first volume. Luisa's mystical experiences unveil an interconnectedness, whereby those living in the Divine Will can alleviate the sufferings of purgatorial souls through their prayers and sacrifices. It hearkens back to the church's longstanding traditions of intercessory prayer for the faithful departed, thus reinforcing the communal aspects of salvation.

Lastly, the revelations present an archetype for the New Era of Sanctity, foretelling a time when humanity will live in perfect harmony with divine mandates. This anticipation of a renewed earth is not merely eschatological but serves as a present calling to imbue current existence with virtues that prefigure the heavenly reign of God's Will.

In their entirety, these revelations insist that we are not passive recipients but active participants in God's divine economy. They prompt a reevaluation of our spiritual lives, urging an intimate and transformative union with the Will of God. Thus, Volume 1 invites its believers to embark upon a journey of mystical depth and theological richness, making manifest the divine desire to draw all into the circle of His Will.

Such eloquent affirmations intertwine to form a tapestry of grace, on which the Divine Will sketches His loving plan for each soul. This volume serves not just to edify but to elevate, making every revelation an invitation to a higher plane of holiness.

Chapter 6: Summarizing Volume 2 Of The Book Of Heaven

As we delve into the profound depths of Volume 2 of The Book of Heaven, we encounter a continuation of the celestial dialogues and divine instructions bestowed upon Luisa Piccarreta. This volume illuminates the grandeur of God's eternal Will and His desire for Its reign within our souls. Through intricate revelations and sublime visions, Luisa is taken deeper into the mysteries of Divine Love and the reparative mission assigned to her. Revelations within this volume emphasize the importance of living in Divine Will as a means to restore the original holiness intended for humanity, thus bringing forth a union with Heaven itself. Each key theme, gracefully woven through the celestial whispers, beckons us to surrender our entire being to the Divine Volition, for in such a surrender lies the secret to divine fruitfulness and the fulfillment of God's majestic plan for His creation.

Key Themes

As we embark upon the profound journey of Volume 2 of The Book of Heaven, the splendor of the Divine Will unfurls in myriad dimensions. The key themes that define this volume are intricate, imbued with celestial wisdom, and are paramount to understanding the Divine Will Movement. They beckon the heart and soul towards a deeper communion with the Divine, elucidating the path of divine intentionality woven into the fabric of everyday life.

Foremost among these themes is the sublime Union with God. This is not a mere symbolic relationship but a profound and mystical union wherein the soul is invited into the innermost recesses of God's Will. This theme exemplifies a transformative devotion, elevating the soul's purpose beyond mortal confines and into a divine harmony. It invites the faithful to surrender wholly to God's Will, thus participating in His eternal plan.

Another critical theme is the profound journey of Spiritual Growth and Purification. Volume 2 accentuates the necessity of inner purification, urging believers to shed their earthly attachments and sins. This purification paves the way for the sanctification of the soul, allowing it to reflect the divine light more purely. Through Luisa Piccarreta's dialogues with Christ, readers are provided a roadmap for navigating their spiritual trials and tribulations, with divine grace as their compass.

The theme of Divine Cooperation embarks on a riveting exploration of the symbiotic relationship between human will and Divine Will. It extols the virtues of actively cooperating with God's Will in everyday tasks. This cooperation is not passive but an active engagement that transforms ordinary actions into divine acts, thereby sanctifying each moment. It instills a sense of divine purpose and underscores the importance of living in constant alignment with God's desires.

Witnessing the Divine Providence in life's minutiae forms another pivotal theme. This theme enraptures the essence of God's omnipresent hand in every element of creation. It offers a serene assurance that every facet of life, from momentous events to seemingly insignificant details, is orchestrated by divine providence. This understanding cultivates a trustful surrender, where believers can rest in the knowledge that nothing escapes the purview of God's benevolent design.

Integral to the teachings of Volume 2 is the Call to Universal Holiness. This theme reiterates that the call to holiness is not limited to a select few but is a universal vocation. It promises that through living in the Divine Will, every soul, regardless of its state in life, can attain a profound communion with God. This democratization of holiness challenges believers to embrace their spiritual potential without reservations.

The Battle Against Evil is an enduring theme that threads through Volume 2, where believers are reminded of the ever-present spiritual warfare between good and evil. Luisa's revelations often dwell on the importance of vigilance, prayer, and sacramental life as fortresses against the forces of darkness. It is a clarion call to spiritual warriors, emphasizing that victory in this battle is assured for those who remain steadfast in the Divine Will.

Additionally, the theme of Redeeming Suffering takes center stage, illustrating how personal trials can be offered for the redemption of souls. Luisa teaches that suffering, when united with Christ's passion, becomes a powerful conduit for grace. This understanding provides immense solace, transforming suffering into a sacrificial act of love that participates in Christ's redemptive mission.

The Promise of the Coming Reign of the Divine Will fills the pages with an eschatological hope. It assures the faithful of a future where God's Will shall reign supreme on earth as in heaven. This promise stokes the flames of faith, urging believers to be harbingers of this divine era through their present lives. It is a vision that captivates the imagination, fortifying the soul with hope and anticipation.

The Sacredness of Work is another notable theme, propounding that every labor, when performed in alignment with the Divine Will, becomes an act of worship. This sanctifies the mundane and elevates daily toil to divine service. Luisa's teachings imbue ordinary work with extraordinary significance, encouraging believers to seek divine purpose in their vocations.

Furthermore, the theme of Eucharistic Centrality resonates deeply throughout Volume 2. The Eucharist is portrayed as the summit of divine communion—the source and summit of the Christian life. Luisa's revelations beckon the faithful to cherish the Eucharist as the wellspring of divine grace and strength. It is both a cornerstone and a capstone of a life aligned with God's Will.

An evocative theme of Childlike Trust emerges, inviting believers to embrace a trusting dependence on God, reminiscent of a child's trust in a loving parent. This trust is the foundation of a serene and confident faith, unencumbered by the anxieties of the world. It is a call to abandon oneself to divine providence with the innocence and simplicity of a child.

The recurring motif of Marian Devotion provides a tender and maternal guidance for living in the Divine Will. Mary, as the perfect exemplar of surrender to God's Will, offers a model for the faithful. Her fiat is extolled as the ultimate act of compliance with Divine Will, and her intercession is sought as a means to achieve such surrender.

Moreover, the theme of Intercessory Prayer underscores the pow'r and necessity of praying for others. Luisa's revelations affirm that prayer, particularly when aligned with God's Will, can bring about transformative graces and conversions. It calls the faithful to become intercessors, echoing Christ's own mediatory role.

The pages also teem with the theme of the Mystical Body of Christ, wherein each believer's life is intertwined with the lives of all in the communion of saints. It fosters a sense of spiritual solidarity and collective sanctification, reinforcing that each act of virtue or vice resonates throughout the entire mystical body.

Lastly, the theme of Continuous Divine Presence envelops the reader in the assurance of God's unceasing companionship. It teaches that through living in the Divine Will, one experiences a perpetual communion with God, transcending the temporal distinctions of time and space. This continual presence provides a constant source of divine strength and joy.

In summation, the key themes of Volume 2 of The Book of Heaven provide a comprehensive tapestry of divine teachings that beckon the soul towards a fuller participation in God's Will. They are not mere concepts but lived realities, inviting each soul to delve into the depths of divine intimacy and eternal purpose. These themes collectively paint a portrait of a life fully surrendered to, and imbued with, the Divine Will, promising a foretaste of heavenly communion on earth.

Notable Revelations

In the labyrinth of celestial wisdom found within Volume 2 of "The Book of Heaven," certain revelations stand paramount, shimmering like the stars glistening in the midnight sky. These divine disclosures unveil a panorama of the Almighty's grandeur, displaying the intricate tapestry of His Divine Will in ways heretofore unimagined. One cannot delve into this volume without encountering profound spiritual insights that elucidate God's ineffable designs for humanity.

Foremost among these revelations is the notion of living in the Divine Will as a foretaste of the beatific vision. Unlike the mere observance of God's commandments, this is an invitation to partake directly in the divine life, akin to the experience of the saints in heaven. Such a state transcends ordinary sanctity, urging the faithful into an intimate union with God that surpasses the soul's highest aspirations. Indeed, to live in the Divine Will is to envelop oneself in the very desires and operations of the Creator, molding one's own will entirely with His.

Moreover, Volume 2 illuminates the radical concept of sanctification as not merely human effort but divine action. Luisa conveys that sanctity, in its truest form, is the work of God within us, transforming us into living tabernacles of His presence. This is not an endeavor accomplished solely through human striving but through an acquiescence to His divine activity. Here, the soul learns to be a passive recipient of grace, allowing the Almighty to sculpt from its raw material a masterpiece of sanctity.

Another striking revelation concerns the continuous act. Unlike actions bound by time's constraints, these continuous acts are perpetual offerings to God, echoing the eternal now. Such acts, when performed in the Divine Will, resonate eternally, magnifying their merit and reaping immeasurable spiritual fruit. Luisa's accounts vividly illustrate how every heartbeat, every breath, when united with Christ, takes on ineffable value and infinite significance.

Integral to this Volume's revelations is the transformative power of divine love. Love, in the Divine Will, is not a mere sentiment but an act of the will, united with God's own love. This divine love purifies, elevates, and sanctifies the soul, drawing it ever deeper into the embrace of the Eternal Father. Through this celestial love, the soul participates in the divine economy of salvation, offering sacrifices of great worth for the benefit of all humanity.

Luisa further reveals the astonishing power of suffering when embraced in union with Christ. Sufferings, be they great or small, assume a redemptive quality when willingly accepted in the Divine Will. They become instruments of grace, both for the individual soul and for the world at large. In this light, suffering is transformed from a burden to a precious gift, a means of intimate participation in the Paschal Mystery of Christ.

Equally revolutionary is the understanding of human acts as seeds sown in the Divine Will, destined to bear eternal fruit. Every act, whether mundane or extraordinary, when performed in union with the Divine Will, contributes to the establishment of God's Kingdom on earth. Such an understanding infuses daily life with profound purpose and significance, inviting every believer to become a co-architect in the divine plan of salvation.

The revelations also delve into the role of creation in the divine order. Nature, Luisa explains, is a manifestation of God's love, a symphony of praise orchestrated by the Creator. Human beings, when living in the Divine Will, are called to join this cosmic chorus, giving voice to creation's silent adoration. In this perspective, the natural world is not merely a backdrop to human life but a fundamental part of the divine liturgy.

Furthermore, the notion of divine timing emerges with riveting clarity. God's actions, as revealed to Luisa, occur in what she calls the "divine timing," a sacred tempo perfectly orchestrated for the fulfillment of His will. This divine timing transcends human understanding and invites the faithful to trust in God's providence, even when His plans seem inscrutable. Such trust becomes a bedrock virtue, anchoring the soul in the assurance of divine wisdom.

These revelations also underscore the primacy of humility in the spiritual life. True humility, as illuminated in Volume 2, is not mere self-effacement but a profound acknowledgment of one's dependence on God. It is the soul's recognition of its own nothingness and the omnipotence of the Divine Will. This humility becomes a conduit for grace, opening the heart wide to receive the fullness of God's benevolent outpouring.

An additional notable revelation involves the intercession of the saints and angels. Luisa describes their active and passionate involvement in the lives of those striving to live in the Divine Will. These celestial beings, she reveals, are ever eager to assist, guide, and protect, acting as divine emissaries and helpers in the grand adventure of sanctity. Their presence brings comfort and courage, assuring the faithful that they are never alone in their spiritual journey.

Similarly, we find valuable insights into the transformative power of divine truth. Luisa articulates how truth is not only a set of doctrines but a living reality that shapes and forms the soul. Embracing divine truth is a dynamic process that involves the intellect, the heart, and the will, leading to a profound conformity with Christ, who is Truth incarnate.

Moreover, Volume 2 speaks profoundly of the Eucharistic life. The revelations cast new light on the Mystery of the Eucharist, portraying it as the fountainhead of divine life and the center of the Divine Will. Luisa explains that the Eucharist is not merely a sacrament to be received but a reality to be lived, infusing every aspect of the believer's life with divine grace. Each communion becomes an intimate encounter with the living Christ, fortifying the soul and drawing it deeper into the epicenter of divine love.

In conclusion, the revelations of Volume 2 of "The Book of Heaven" present an unparalleled vista of divine wisdom, calling the faithful to a life of extraordinary union with God's Divine Will. As we ponder these revelations, our hearts are drawn to more fervently seek this divine union, our minds illumined by the celestial light that emanates from Luisa Piccarreta's writings. Indeed, these revelations are not only notable but transformative, inviting each soul into the ineffable mystery of living in God's eternal and glorious Will.

Chapter 7: Summarizing Volume 3 Of The Book Of Heaven

In the third volume of The Book of Heaven, the Divine Will, like a gorgeous tapestry, reveals yet another layer of its celestial grandeur. Herein, Luisa Piccarreta delves deeper into the sacred interplay between human free will and the Divine Fiat, elucidating how aligned souls can attain sanctity through the Divine Volition. Heavenly dialogues between Jesus and Luisa weave intricate themes of surrender, love, and divine intimacy, emphasizing the transformative power of living in God's Will. Distinct revelations illuminate the profound harmony that unfolds when one's own will ceases to resist the Divine's gentle yet firm guidance. Through these teachings, one perceives the fruitfulness of allowing the Divine Will to permeate every facet of human existence, manifesting a foretaste of heavenly bliss on earth. Thus, Volume 3 stands as an epic testament to the potency and depth of God's eternal plan, inviting the faithful to embrace their role in the grand divine symphony.

Key Themes

The third volume of "The Book of Heaven" unfurls as a tapestry replete with themes that illuminate the grandeur and subtlety of the Divine Will. Here, the threads of heaven's intentions weave through the life of Luisa Piccarreta, emphasizing profound notions that warrant veneration and reflection among devout Roman Catholics.

In this volume, the paramount theme is the intimate union of the soul with God's Will. This union transcends mere compliance; it delves into the transformative power of divine servitude. The writings paint a vivid picture of the soul's journey towards embracing the Divine Will wholly, not as a detached observer but as an active participant. The narrative underscores the grace that flows when the human will is surrendered to the divine, a surrender that ushers in a celestial harmony.

An additional theme that rises to prominence in Volume 3 is the sanctification of daily life. Through her divine communications, Luisa presents a vision wherein every mundane act, when performed in union with God's Will, becomes an act of worship. This concept elevates the ordinary to the extraordinary, suggesting that the path to sanctity is not confined to grand gestures or overtly religious acts but permeates every aspect of one's existence.

The narrative further explores the theme of suffering in union with Christ. Luisa's revelations often spring from a place of profound physical and spiritual suffering, yet this suffering is portrayed not as an end but a means. It is through such trials that one is sculpted and refined, aligning more closely with the likeness of Christ. The notion of 'participatory suffering' echoes through the text, offering solace and purpose to those who bear their crosses in the light of divine grace.

One cannot overlook the theme of divine mercy that pervades this volume. The love and compassion of God, constantly seeking the redemption and sanctification of His creatures, shine through Luisa's writings. Her words echo the boundless mercy that awaits those who seek refuge in the Divine Will. This theme is a clarion call to return to the fold, to embrace the infinite love that the Creator extends towards His creation.

A frequent undercurrent throughout the third volume is that of eschatological urgency. Luisa's messages often carry an implicit, sometimes explicit, sense of the approaching fulfillment of divine plans. Her communications encourage the faithful to awaken to their spiritual responsibilities, realigning their lives according to the divine blueprint. This theme evokes a sense of urgency, nudging the reader toward a more vigilant and faithful adherence to God's Will.

The theme of divine revelation itself is examined thoroughly. Luisa provides a window into the continuous dialogue between heaven and earth, unfolding not in grandiose proclamations but in the quiet, persistent whispers of divine love. Such revelations reiterate the ongoing nature of God's communication with His people, affirming that heaven is not distant or silent but everpresent and involved in the minutiae of human existence.

Interwoven with the rich theological insights is the recurring theme of trust in divine providence. Luisa's recollections emphasize a steadfast trust in God's plan, even when the path is shrouded in uncertainty and doubt. This trust is the anchor for the soul navigating the tumultuous seas of life, a beacon of light that guides one towards the safe harbor of divine communion.

Volume 3 also touches upon the collective responsibility of believers in manifesting the Divine Will on earth. It suggests a communal dimension to personal holiness, highlighting the ripple effects of individual acts of divine conformity. It elaborates on the idea that the sanctity of one can uplift the spiritual climate of many, reinforcing the interconnectedness of the mystical body of Christ.

A theme of reparation and intercession surfaces with poignant clarity. Luisa's writings urge the faithful to engage in acts of reparation for the sins of the world. These acts are not merely penitential but are seen as powerful means of aligning one's will with that of the Redeemer, participating actively in the redemptive mission of Christ.

Furthermore, the exploration of the virtues cultivated by living in the Divine Will becomes a central pillar of this volume. It illuminates virtues such as humility, patience, and charity, showing how they flourish when nourished by divine grace. These virtues are positioned not as distant ideals but as attainable possibilities for those who earnestly seek to live in God's Will.

Lastly, the theme of discipleship permeates Luisa's writings in Volume 3. She underscores the call to become true disciples of Christ, inviting others to embark on a journey that might be demanding but is unequivocally rewarding. Discipleship, as portrayed here, is about embodying the teachings of Christ through the transformative power of living in the Divine Will.

Through these key themes, Volume 3 of "The Book of Heaven" presents a rich and multi-faceted exploration of the spiritual life aimed at fostering a deeper union with God's Will. It serves as both a guide and a challenge to the faithful, inviting them to step into a more profound relationship with the Divine, thus realizing the fullness of the Christian vocation.

Notable Revelations

The third volume of The Book of Heaven unveils a series of extraordinary divine insights, each more profound than the last. Within these pages, Luisa Piccarreta delves deeper into the mystical realms, where heaven meets earth in the most subtle and sublime of encounters. A notable revelation in this volume, transcending mere earthly wisdom, centers upon the profound unity and synchronicity between the human will and the Divine Will. The text expounds upon the idea that one's soul may find its true liberation and ultimate fulfillment only when it fully subsumes its desires into God's eternal will.

One of the most striking revelations documented in this volume involves the luminous truth behind the Eucharistic presence. Luisa relates that in the sacrament of the Eucharist, Jesus not only shares his body and blood but also yearns to unite His Divine Will with the human will. This unity is described as the pinnacle of divine intimacy, transforming the soul into a living tabernacle of divine grace. Such revelations offer a fresh lens through which the faithful may contemplate this cornerstone of Catholic worship, thus increasing devotion and reverence.

Furthermore, this volume brings to light the transformative power of suffering when united with Christ's Passion. Luisa's revelations echo the theology of redemptive suffering, emphasizing that every sorrow borne with love and offered up to God holds an eternal value. Each tear, each pang, echoes in heaven, contributing to the salvation of souls. By understanding this divine economy of suffering, Catholics are given a fortified framework within which to perceive their trials, transforming pain into instruments of divine grace.

A salient aspect of these revelations is the augmenting role of the Blessed Virgin Mary. She appears not only as the mother of Jesus but as the quintessential model of living in the Divine Will. Through various visions and celestial dialogues, Luisa unveils Mary's profound relationship with the Holy Trinity, her immaculate reception of the Divine Will, and her steadfast role as an intercessor. This insight brings a fresh perspective to Marian devotion, inviting believers to emulate her unwavering submission to God's plan.

Another monumental revelation is the unveiling of the "Rounds of Creation." These divine reflections elucidate how the entirety of creation is an immense cathedral, where every created element, from the stars in the firmament to the smallest blade of grass, sings a hymn of praise to the Creator. The faithful are encouraged to participate in these rounds, offering back to God the love and adoration imbued in every aspect of creation. This revelatory practice can deeply enrich one's spiritual life, fostering a cosmic sense of connection with both the Creator and creation.

Volume 3 also highlights the nature of sanctity in the Divine Will, presenting it not as a distant, unattainable ideal but as a lived reality accessible to every soul. Luisa reveals how even the simplest acts, when performed in union with God's will, acquire an immeasurable divine value. This understanding democratizes holiness, showing that sainthood is not confined to the ascetic or the extraordinary but can flourish in the ordinariness of daily life.

One cannot overlook the eschatological dimensions of the revelations in this volume. While the previous volumes shone light predominantly on the present transformative power of the Divine Will, Volume 3 also peers into the future promises awaiting those who live immersed in God's Will. These promises include not just personal beatitude but a renewal of the entire cosmos, a new creation where God's Will reigns supreme in all hearts. Such eschatological revelations anchor hope in the visceral promise of divine justice and eternal harmony.

Profound indeed is the revelation concerning the importance of human cooperation with divine grace. By aligning one's will with the Divine, individuals can partake in the co-creative work of God, bringing His kingdom ever closer to its fulfillment. This partnership extends beyond mere passive reception; it is an active, dynamic engagement, urging believers to live out their faith with an evangelical zeal and fervor, contributing to the spiritual and moral renewal of the world.

Moreover, Volume 3 touches upon the theme of divine providence in a way that enriches the understanding of God's intimate involvement in human affairs. According to the revelations, every event, be it joyful or sorrowful, is intricately woven into God's redemptive plan. Trusting in divine providence thus becomes an act of faith and a testament to one's abandonment to God's guiding hand. This enriches the Catholic tradition of surrendering to God's will with a nuanced appreciation for His infinite wisdom and benevolence.

Lastly, the volume underscores the pivotal role of the Divine Will in engendering true peace, both within the soul and in the world at large. According to Luisa's revelations, only by living in harmony with God's Will can individuals and communities overcome division, strife, and discord. This divine peace is not merely the absence of conflict but a profound inner tranquility that emanates from a heart completely attuned to the heartbeat of God. Such a revelation offers both a personal and communal path to achieving the harmony that reflects the Kingdom of Heaven on earth.

In summation, the Notable Revelations of Volume 3 build a magnificent tapestry of divine wisdom, each thread woven with the subtleties of celestial nuance. They collectively call every believer to a deeper embrace of the Divine Will, a fuller participation in the sacramental life, and a higher aspiration towards living sanctified lives in union with God's eternal plan. This volume, rich in spiritual insights and practical applications, stands as an eloquent testament to the everlasting fruits bore by the Divine Will Movement, affirming its place within the sacred traditions of the Catholic Church.

Chapter 8: Summarizing Volume 4 Of The Book Of Heaven

In Volume 4 of "The Book of Heaven," the divine wisdom imparted upon Luisa Piccarreta reveals the profound depths of God's love and the eternal significance of living in His Divine Will. This volume weaves together celestial visions and intimate dialogues with the Divine, which convey the intricate dance between human will and God's supreme plan. Key themes emerge, illustrating how the soul, when surrendered to God's Will, ascends to a higher state of spiritual communion and fulfillment. Notable revelations underscore the transformative power of divine grace and the sacrificial love mirrored in Christ's Passion, drawing a parallel to Luisa's own spiritual journey. Emphasizing both simplicity and grandeur, these teachings beckon the faithful to a deeper understanding and practice of embracing God's Will, thereby joining in the eternal liturgy of heaven itself. Indeed, Volume 4 stands as a testament to the divine orchestration of salvation and sanctification through God's omnipotent Will.

Key Themes

The profundity inherent in Volume 4 of "The Book of Heaven" ascends to celestial heights with themes that encapsulate the very heart of Divine Will theology. Foremost among these is an unyielding focus on the omnipotence and omnipresence of God's will in the life of his faithful servant, Luisa Piccarreta. The volume emphasizes the transcendence of God's will over human frailty, positing that the Divine Will is the fount from which all life, decisions, and actions must spring forth.

This volume illuminates how trust and obedience serve as indispensable pillars for living in the Divine Will. Luisa's experiences reiterate that unwavering trust in God's providence transforms the believer's soul, enabling it to align seamlessly with the Divine Will. The narrative extols a surrender so complete, it mirrors the abandonment Christ himself exhibited in Gethsemane, imploring not his own will but the Father's.

A theme that resounds through these revelations is the sanctity of suffering when united with God's Will. Suffering, perceived through human lenses as a bane, is herein elevated to a sacramental dimension. Luisa's afflictions become divine touches, marks of favor rather than scorn. Volume 4 thus invites believers to reinterpret pain and adversity as participatory gestures in Christ's own Passion, transforming tribulation into sanctification.

An inextricable interweaving of human and divine wills manifests in the recurrent theme of spiritual union. The heart of this notion lies in a mystical tethering to the Sacred Heart of Jesus. Through this union, Luisa receives clarity and fortitude, asserting that human limitations dissolve when immersed in Divine Love. Hence, Volume 4 calls the faithful to merge their will with the Divine, comprising a spiritual symphony pierced by the melodies of eternal love.

Furthermore, the paternal aspect of God is emphasized, underscoring a loving and nurturing relationship with humanity. Instead of a remote, austere deity, God is portrayed as a caring Father, intimately involved in the minutiae of his children's lives. This fatherly presence invites readers into a closer, more affectionate walk with the Creator, dismantling the barriers of fear and misunderstanding.

The theme of divine pedagogy is another hallmark of Volume 4. God's revelations to Luisa serve a didactic purpose, aiming to instruct and elevate the understanding of the Divine Will. This pedagogical approach is both gentle and transformative, crafting a spiritual formation that prepares souls for eternity. Each lesson, inscribed upon Luisa's heart, is intended to be a beacon for all who seek the path of righteousness.

Moreover, Volume 4 accentuates the indispensability of prayer and contemplation. The revelations assert that prayer, rooted in the Divine Will, transcends mere words and becomes a powerful conduit for divine grace. Through concentrated prayer, believers commune with God, drawing heavenly wisdom and strength for their earthly pilgrimage.

A paramount theme is the manifestation of divine love through practical acts of charity. Luisa's voluminous writings on the Divine Will are not abstract musings but directives for tangible love in action. This theme inspires the faithful to view each act of kindness as a reflection of God's infinite love, thereby turning ordinary deeds into extraordinary channels of divine mercy.

Additionally, the revelations underscore the comprehensive harmony between the Divine Will and Sacred Tradition. Volume 4 skillfully aligns its divine insights with the enduring truths of Church teachings, ensuring a harmonious coexistence that venerates tradition while embracing divine innovation. This convergence stands as a testament to the movement's orthodoxy, alleviating fears of doctrinal conflict.

The theme of eschatological hope is also pronounced within this volume. Luisa's encounters reveal a divine roadmap towards the fulfillment of cosmic redemption, offering the faithful glimpses of the divine parousia. This eschatological vision cements a hopeful expectation that God's kingdom will ultimately reign, affirming that current sufferings are but transient preludes to eternal glory.

Another salient theme is the integral role of humility. The revelations extol humility as the gateway to divine intimacy, portraying it as a virtuosity of the highest degree. Luisa's life embodies this humility, as she submits herself entirely to God's Will, thus becoming a vessel of divine action. This theme impels the faithful to seek humility, knowing it purifies the soul and opens hearts to divine mysteries.

The celestial radiance of love forms the very marrow of Volume 4, stressing that divine affection must flow unabated through the believer's life. Love here is not merely an emotion but a divine attribute the faithful must cultivate. It's an active force, energizing and ennobling every aspect of human existence.

Last but not least, the theme of divine providence pervades the narrative. Luisa's writings emphasize that nothing escapes the attentive gaze of God. Every moment, every trial is an orchestrated part of God's majestic symphony. This theme assures the faithful that divine foresight governs all events, transforming fears into trust and anxiety into peace.

The volume serves as an expansive testament to the inexorable pull of God's love and will. It offers a sweeping yet intimate view of divine-human interplay, encouraging the faithful to rise to the divine summons. The key themes woven through Volume 4 build a robust theological framework, inviting believers into a deeper, more committed relationship with the Divine Will.

In heralding these timeless themes, Volume 4 of "The Book of Heaven" stands as an indomitable beacon of divine wisdom. It challenges, nourishes, and guides the faithful into the embrace of God's eternal and all-encompassing will, laying the groundwork for a life brimming with divine purpose and celestial joy.

Notable Revelations

In Volume 4 of "The Book of Heaven," one finds an outpouring of divine wisdom, graciously imparted unto Luisa Piccarreta. The revelations contained therein stand as beacons of heavenly light, illuminating the path towards a deeper union with the Divine Will. They are not mere concepts but living truths, resplendent with God's love, that beckon the faithful to embrace a life of full surrender to His holy will.

Among the revelations, one most striking vision reveals the extraordinary intimacy that God seeks with His creations. The Lord confides to Luisa that His Will is not a distant decree but an intimate embrace, an indwelling presence yearning to animate every thought, word, and action of mankind. Such revelations stir the soul to an awareness of God's immeasurable desire to dwell within us as active co-participants in His divine plan.

Furthermore, the revelations underscore the infinite power and efficacy of God's Will. Through vivid illustrations and profound metaphors, Luisa is shown how the Divine Will operates as the sovereign force behind all creation, harmonizing the cosmos with perfect order and beauty. The faithful are called to recognize this supreme dominion and yield fully to it, thereby partaking in its creative and redemptive power.

A poignant disclosure details Christ's suffering, not only in His Passion but also in His continual grief over mankind's refusal to live in accordance with His Will. In such moments, the reader encounters a Christ who suffers anew in every soul that rejects His love. This revelation invites a deeper compassion and solidarity with the suffering Christ, prompting believers to heal His wounds through their fidelity to the Divine Will.

The necessity of reparation and sacrifice is another essential theme. Luisa is often depicted performing acts of immense spiritual value, uniting her sufferings with Christ's own. Through these acts, the message is clear: every soul is called to participate in the redemptive work of Christ, offering their daily crosses in union with His perfect Sacrifice.

The revelations also delve deeply into the mystery of the Eucharist. Christ reveals to Luisa the unimaginable graces that flow from the Blessed Sacrament, emphasizing its role as the sustenance of those living in the Divine Will. This sacramental life is portrayed as the means by which the soul is continually nourished and fortified, allowing the Divine Will to take deeper root within.

In one awe-inspiring vision, the Blessed Virgin Mary is presented as the epitome of living in the Divine Will. She stands as a radiant exemplar, showcasing the heights of sanctity attainable when one fully embraces this divine gift. The faithful are called to emulate her unwavering fiat, thereby allowing the Divine Will to accomplish wonders in their own lives.

Moreover, the revelations invite a profound trust in Divine Providence. Time and again, Luisa is reassured of God's meticulous care and wisdom, governing all events and circumstances.

This trust is not passive but active, urging believers to abandon themselves to God's designs with serene confidence and unshakeable faith.

The communications also elaborate on the celestial harmony and peace promised to those who live in the Divine Will. These souls are assured of a foretaste of heavenly bliss here on earth, as their wills become perfectly united with God's, creating an interior paradise where divine joy reigns supreme.

Through these powerful revelations, the faithful are instructed in the virtues necessary for living in the Divine Will. They learn the paramount importance of humility, patience, and charity, which soften the heart and open it to the inflow of divine grace. Such virtues are not presented as mere moral ideals but as practical paths to deep spiritual transformation.

The dialogic nature of the revelations between Luisa and Jesus unveils a tender and affectionate relationship, full of divine solicitude and care. These interactions reflect the closeness that God desires with each soul, emboldening the believer to cultivate a personal, loving relationship with the Divine Will.

Lastly, the revelations reveal the eschatological dimension of the Divine Will. Luisa is shown glimpses of the ultimate fulfillment of God's plan, where the Divine Will reigns supreme in a renewed creation. This vision instills hope and a forward-looking anticipation, encouraging the faithful to persevere in their spiritual journey with eyes fixed on the promised glory.

Volume 4, in its richness, thus stands not merely as a collection of divine insights but as a clarion call to the faithful. It beckons each soul with the promise of profound intimacy with the Divine, urging a life wholly immersed in God's holy and eternal Will. Such a life, as unveiled through Luisa's revelations, is nothing less than a foretaste of Heaven itself.

Chapter 9: Summarizing Volume 5 Of The Book Of Heaven

The celestial opus of Volume 5 of the Book of Heaven unveils a divine tapestry woven with the luminous threads of God's will and His profound love for humanity. In this volume, Luisa Piccarreta's revelations ascend the spiritual ladder, granting us insights into the transformative power of living fully immersed in the Divine Will. Channeling the sacred essence of our Lord's teachings, the revelations herein emphasize the paramount importance of continuous union with God's will, seeking to align every thought, word, and deed with His eternal plan. Through poignant dialogues and spiritual experiences, Luisa illuminates the path to sanctity, guiding souls toward an existence that reflects the very heart of Christ's sacrificial love. As we delve into the pearlescent depths of Volume 5, the omnipotence of divine love and the imperative call to live within its embrace are laid bare, offering a beacon of hope and a testament to the fruitfulness that such a life, deeply enshrined in divine grace, inevitably reaps.

Key Themes

In Volume 5 of The Book of Heaven, myriad themes emerge that knit together a profound tapestry of divine revelation, prodigious love, and the intricate workings of God's Will. Each theme, as meticulously chronicled by Luisa Piccarreta, embodies the essence of her encounters with the Divine and exudes spiritual profundity. They invite the reader to delve deeper into the mysteries of faith and embrace the transformative power of the Divine Will. These themes are not mere philosophical musings but profound insights meant to guide the faithful towards a more intimate union with the Creator.

Foremost among the themes is the unfathomable Love of God. The Love portrayed in Volume 5 transcends human comprehension, painting a picture of a Creator whose love is boundless, unwavering, and eternally seeking the good of the soul. This divine love is an invitation to reciprocate with a love that mirrors the divine, fostering a relationship grounded in trust and surrender. The message is clear: God desires to be loved with the same intensity He loves, creating an unbreakable bond between the Creator and the created.

Another theme that pulsates through the pages of this volume is the centrality of the Divine Will. Luisa receives the sacred understanding that the fulfillment of one's life lies in the perfect conformity to the Will of God. It's a call to abandon personal desires and to embrace the Divine Will as the ultimate guide. This surrender is not seen as a relinquishment of freedom, but rather as a pathway to true liberation and divine intimacy. The Divine Will becomes the compass that directs every thought, word, and action towards the divine purpose.

The notion of suffering, intertwined with redemption, is also profoundly articulated. Suffering, in the Divine Will, is not viewed as a mere consequence of a fallen world but as a necessary participation in the redemptive mission of Christ. Luisa's sufferings, as revealed to her, become a means of sanctification and a conduit through which God's graces flow into the world. This noble acceptance of suffering is not embraced in despair but in joyful submission, recognizing it as a powerful tool for spiritual growth and the salvation of souls.

Additionally, the theme of humility resonates deeply. Luisa's writings elucidate that true greatness in the Kingdom of God is found in humility and meekness. This humility is not a form of self-deprecation but a recognition of one's utter dependence on God's grace. The humble soul is exalted, for it is in humility that one becomes most receptive to the divine workings and inspirations. Through her own example, Luisa embodies the virtue of humility, offering herself as an unassuming instrument of God's revelations.

Fidelity to the Divine Will is another key theme echoed throughout Volume 5. This fidelity is presented as a steadfast commitment to live in accordance with God's desires, even in the face of trials and temptations. It is through this unwavering fidelity that the soul remains anchored in divine grace and becomes a beacon of God's light in a darkened world. The writings stress that such fidelity requires constant vigilance, prayer, and an unwavering trust in God's providence.

The interplay between creation and the Creator is also notably conveyed. Luisa's writings reveal a unique relationship between mankind and the entire creation, all harmonizing within the Divine Will. Creation, as an expression of God's grandeur, invites the soul to partake in its beauty and to recognize the divine imprints embedded within it. This perspective elevates the mundane to the sacred, encouraging a profound reverence for all of God's creations.

Sanctification is another vital theme. Luisa often reflects upon the call to holiness as a universal vocation. Sanctification, in her revelations, is not an abstract concept but a practical daily pursuit. It requires the soul to integrate the Divine Will into every aspect of life, transforming ordinary actions into acts of divine worship. This transformative process leads the soul into a closer union with God, striving towards the perfection that He desires.

The theme of divine providence weaves through the pages with elegance. Luisa's experiences underscore a deep trust in God's providential care. Even in the midst of uncertainties and adversities, the writings encourage an unwavering confidence in God's perfect plan. Divine providence reassures the soul that nothing occurs outside the scope of God's wisdom and benevolence, thus fostering a spirit of peace and contentment.

Closely aligned with providence is the theme of divine wisdom. Volume 5 explicates the boundless wisdom of God that orchestrates all events in accordance with His divine plan. This wisdom invites the soul to surrender its limited understanding and to trust in the all-encompassing intelligence of the Creator. The revelations encourage seeking divine wisdom through prayer, contemplation, and an intimate relationship with God.

Intercession emerges as a powerful theme, highlighting the role of the faithful in praying for the world. Luisa's revelations emphasize the importance of intercessory prayer, underscoring its efficacy in drawing down God's grace and mercy. The faithful are called to become intercessors, lifting up the needs of others and the world, trusting that God will respond with divine generosity.

Unity with Christ is central to the spiritual journey. Luisa's encounters reflect a deep yearning for an intimate, unbroken communion with Christ. This unity is not merely symbolic but a lived reality where the soul becomes one with the heart and mission of Christ. Through this unity, the soul participates in the redemptive work of Jesus, offering itself as a vessel through which His love and mercy flow.

The theme of obedience resonates strongly, portraying it as an indispensable virtue in living out the Divine Will. Obedience, as revealed to Luisa, is an expression of love and trust in God. It is through obedience that the soul aligns itself with divine commands, thus fostering a harmonious relationship with God. The writings convey that true freedom is found in obedient submission to God's Will.

Furthermore, the role of the Holy Spirit is poignantly highlighted. The Holy Spirit is depicted as the divine aid that enlightens, guides, and empowers the soul to live in accord with the Divine Will. Luisa's writings often refer to the inspirations and movements of the Holy Spirit as essential in the journey towards holiness. The faithful are encouraged to cultivate a deep relationship with the Holy Spirit, seeking His guidance in all things.

Lastly, the theme of eternal life is woven throughout the revelations. Luisa's experiences offer a foretaste of the eternal joy and communion with God that awaits the faithful. The writings present a vision of heaven where the soul, united with God, experiences the fullness of divine love and bliss. This eschatological hope serves as a source of encouragement, motivating the faithful to persevere in their earthly journey.

In conclusion, Volume 5 of The Book of Heaven is suffused with divine themes that beckon the Roman Catholic faithful to a profound spiritual renewal. Each theme, steeped in celestial wisdom, serves as a guiding star, illuminating the path towards a deeper union with the Divine Will.

These themes are not only meant to be contemplated but also lived out, transforming the faithful into

Notable Revelations

The pages of Volume 5 of the Book of Heaven unfurl with revelations so profound, they echo through the corridors of eternity, seeking to illuminate the pathway of every soul yearning for divine intimacy. Foremost among these revelations is the concept of the Divine Will as a ceaseless fountain of grace, flowing unabated through Luisa Piccarreta's spiritual writings. Each message unfurls as a banner of divine truth, urging the faithful to immerse themselves wholly in God's eternal plan.

In the soliloquies granted by our Lord to Luisa, there emerges an explicit articulation of living in God's Divine Will, transcending mere obedience to divine command. These revelations accentuate a state of being where the soul aligns itself so perfectly with the Divine Will that its actions become indistinguishable from those of the Creator. It is here, within this symbiosis, that the eternal dance of grace and human will finds its most exquisite harmony.

An especially poignant revelation in Volume 5 pertains to the nature of suffering and its redemptive qualities. Illuminated within these texts is the profound assertion that human suffering, when united with Christ's own passion, becomes an instrument of sanctification and salvation. This teaching invites believers to a deeper understanding and acceptance of their trials as a participation in the salvific work of Christ Himself.

Moreover, the Book of Heaven elevates the concept of divine love to unparalleled heights, revealing it as the fulcrum upon which the Divine Will pivots. The revelations describe an all-encompassing love that calls humanity to love God with an intensity mirroring that of the angels and saints. This divine admonition is not merely a call to action but a transformation of the soul's very essence, shaping it into an instrument of God's loving providence.

Another key revelation that reverberates through the chapters of Volume 5 is the spiritual imperative of divine abandonment. The texts emphasize a complete surrender to God's Will, urging the faithful to renounce their own desires and ambitions. This surrender is depicted not as a loss, but as a magnificent ascent into the heights of spiritual fulfillment and divine communion.

The notion of divine providence also finds significant elaboration. Through Luisa, it becomes evident that every moment of life, every encounter, every joy, and every sorrow is meticulously woven into the fabric of God's eternal plan. The faithful are thus encouraged to view their lives through the lens of divine orchestration, finding peace in the certitude that all events are underpinned by God's benevolent wisdom.

Volume 5 offers not merely individual revelations but constructs a monumental vision of a life lived in the fullness of divine grace. The messages underscore a celestial paradigm wherein the soul, imbued with the Divine Will, transcends earthly limitations and partakes of divine attributes, leading to a life resplendent with the light of God's eternal love.

Herein also lies a revelation on the communion of saints, providing a profound connective tissue between the earthly and the divine. Luisa's writings suggest that the souls living in the Divine Will become spiritual beacons, linking heaven and earth in an unbroken chain of divine love and grace. This communion transforms the spiritual journey into a collective endeavor, binding together all who seek divine intimacy.

Drawing further from the wellspring of divine wisdom, the texts speak to the transformative power of humility. Humility is not depicted merely as a virtue but as the foundation stone of divine sanctity. It is humility that dissolves the barriers of human pride, paving the way for the Divine Will to operate unhindered within the soul. This revelation underscores the necessity of humble submission as the pathway to divine fulfillment.

Another profound aspect revealed in this volume is the eschatological dimension, where the ultimate fulfillment of the Divine Will aligns with the consummation of all things in Christ. The texts paint a vivid picture of the eschaton as not merely an end of times but the reunion of all creation with the divine source. This revelation instills hope and anticipation, urging the faithful to live in readiness for the final divine embrace.

The essence of prayer, as revealed in Volume 5, also takes on a deeper resonance. Prayer is delineated as an ascent of the soul into the divine realm, a conduit for divine grace, and an act of participatory co-creation with God. This transformative view of prayer encourages believers to cultivate a ceaseless dialogue with the divine, recognizing each prayer as a step closer to divine intimacy.

One cannot overlook the articulate metaphors and divine parables that elucidate the complex theological underpinnings of the Divine Will. Through these literary devices, Luisa illustrates profound truths with the simplicity and beauty that capture the heart and mind. These metaphors serve not just to educate but to elevate, offering a glimpse of the divine reality that transcends human comprehension.

Volume 5's revelations extend a clarion call to every Roman Catholic to embrace a life steeped in the Divine Will. This embrace promises a transformative journey where every moment becomes an act of divine love, every suffering a step towards sanctification, and every prayer a thread in the tapestry of God's eternal grace. Through these revelations, the faithful are invited to partake in a divine mystery that is at once ancient and ever-new, a testament to the unending love and wisdom of our Creator.

Chapter 10: Key Teachings In Later Volumes

As we venture further into the profound depths of the later volumes of "The Book of Heaven," the celestial revelations imparted unto Luisa Piccarreta continue to unfold with ever-greater clarity and divine illumination. These teachings, spanning volumes six through thirty-six, illuminate the path for the faithful to live fully in God's Divine Will, transcending mere human willpower. They invite us into an intimate embrace with the Creator, unveiling the exigency of surrender and trust in Divine Providence. These invaluable volumes delineate the intricacies of merging one's will with God's, detailing practices and attitudes that fortify the soul against the onslaughts of temporal temptations and spiritual languor. Woven with unparalleled divine wisdom, they embolden the believer to seek and cherish the eternal harmony promised by living in the Divine Will. In their pages, one discovers the harmonious echoes of sacred tradition and scriptural foundations, proving that the teachings are not only congruent with but also a sublime extension of our holy faith. Thus, these later volumes stand as testament to the fecundity of Luisa's revelations, enriching the lives of all who ardently pursue the Divine Will.

Highlights From Volumes 6-10

In the sacred annals of Volumes 6-10 of the "Book of Heaven," there unfolds a tapestry of divine revelations that beckon the soul towards the ineffable mysteries of God's Will. These volumes, rich with heavenly wisdom, explore the profound depths of living immersed in the Divine Will, offering a luminous path for the faithful to delve deeper into the spiritual wealth bestowed upon Luisa Piccarreta.

The sixth volume opens a gateway to understanding the intimate connection between the soul and its Creator. It elucidates how living in the Divine Will transforms the soul into a sacred repository of divine light, akin to a pure vessel reflecting the dazzling rays of the Eternal Sun. In this state, the soul is not merely seeking God's Will but becomes an active participant in it. This divine partnership infuses every thought, desire, and action with celestial grace, making the soul a living reflection of God's infinite goodness.

Furthermore, Volume 7 reveals the profound importance of sacrificial love and its pivotal role in the divine economy. The narrative conveys that through the offering of one's hardships and sufferings, united with Jesus' own Passion, the soul becomes a co-redeemer. This redemptive participation underscores the intrinsic value of every suffering borne in submission to the Divine Will. It's an invitation to transcend earthly trials, viewing them as a means to participate in the salvific mission of Christ, thus bringing about a deeper union with the Savior.

As we journey through Volume 8, the revelations pivot toward an exploration of divine peace. This peace is described not as a mere absence of conflict but as a positive presence of God's tranquility, a foretaste of the eternal repose promised to the saints. The divine peace bestowed upon those living in the Divine Will is an unshakable serenity that permeates the soul, empowering it to remain steadfast amidst the vicissitudes of life. This peace, akin to the calm that stilled the tempestuous sea, serves as a beacon of divine presence persevering within the heart.

In Volume 9, the teachings expand to encompass the broader cosmos, revealing the universal scope of the Divine Will. Here, we are reminded that creation itself is a testament to the omnipotent will of God. Each element of creation, from the stars in the heavens to the grains of sand on the shore, is an expression of the Divine Will. The faithful soul is called to recognize this universal harmony and to align its will with the divine order, fostering a sense of interconnectedness with all creation. This cosmic vision inspires an ecological consciousness, urging the faithful to respect and care for the world as an extension of God's Will.

Volume 10, the culmination of this section, delves into the transformative power of divine love. It depicts how immersion in the Divine Will sanctifies the soul, elevating it to partake in God's own sanctity. Love, in this context, is not merely an emotion but a dynamic force that transfigures the human will into divine likeness. This sanctifying love is both a privilege and a responsibility, calling the faithful to embody divine virtues in their daily lives, thus becoming vessels of God's transforming love in a world thirsting for redemption.

To summarize, Volumes 6-10 of the "Book of Heaven" offer a profound exploration of the soul's journey into the heart of the Divine Will. They call the faithful to a deeper understanding and participation in the divine life, inviting them to become co-redeemers with Christ, bearers of divine peace, stewards of creation, and embodiments of sanctifying love. Each revelation is a stepping stone on the path to spiritual transformation, guiding the soul towards its ultimate union with the Divine. These teachings not only illuminate the path of personal sanctity but also encourage a broader vision of cosmic harmony, ushering in a new era of divine comprehension and grace.

Highlights From Volumes 11-20

Volumes 11 through 20 of the "Book of Heaven" unfurl with the magnificence of a divine tapestry, weaving intricate insights and lofty revelations. Each page bristles with heavenly wisdom, portraying a grand panorama of the Divine Will, as it beckons souls into deeper communion with God.

Among the most resplendent highlights is the profound elucidation on the nature of the Divine Will itself. We are ushered into an elevated understanding of how living in the Divine Will transcends mere obedience. It is an active participation in the life of the Holy Trinity, aligning our will so intimately with God's that it becomes indistinguishable from His. Here, the mystical union is no longer the exclusive domain of saints but accessible to every soul yearning to embrace divine intimacy.

Furthermore, these volumes speak at length about the concept of the "Eternal Fiat." This powerful term encapsulates the essence of divine submission and creation. Just as God's Fiat brought forth creation and redemption, so too is humanity called to a personal Fiat, a profound 'yes' to divine providence and love. This invitation is not a momentary act but a continuous living in the light of God's eternal presence, imbued with grace and purpose.

One cannot overlook the persistent theme of sanctification invoked through suffering. These volumes lay bare the transformative power inherent in trials and tribulations. Suffering, when embraced in the Divine Will, is not merely endured but celebrated as a sacred offering that purifies and sanctifies. It is depicted as a channel through which immense graces are poured out, both for the individual soul and for mankind at large.

A particularly poignant aspect is the expanded understanding of Jesus' Passion. The volumes recount not only the historical sufferings of Christ but also extend this suffering into a cosmic dimension. Each soul's participation in the Divine Will is seen as a continuation of Christ's redemptive suffering, creating an unbroken chain of love and sacrifice that transcends time.

Illuminated herein is also the extraordinary relationship between the Blessed Virgin Mary and the Divine Will. These writings extol Mary as the 'Queen of the Divine Will,' whose earthly life was the epitome of living fully in God's Will. She is presented not merely as an intercessor but as a model and guide, leading believers step-by-step into deeper harmony with divine intentions.

The notion of "Divine Acts" becomes a key focal point. Engaging in Divine Acts means performing everyday activities—but within the Divine Will. These acts, however mundane, acquire eternal value and significance. This teaching infuses daily living with a sense of sacred duty and unparalleled spiritual richness.

Adding to the richness of these texts are the depictions of celestial communications. The dialogues between Luisa Piccarreta and Jesus Christ detail profound spiritual insights, elevating mundane realities into the heavenly sphere. These conversations reflect an intimacy that invites believers to foster a similar, unwavering relationship with the Divine.

In Volumes 11 through 20, there is also an undeniable emphasis on the kingdom of the Divine Will, which is envisaged as an impending reality. This kingdom, we learn, is not confined to the afterlife but is meant to be realized here on earth. We are called to be active participants in manifesting this kingdom, thus bringing heaven closer to earth through every act performed in union with God's Will.

The teachings on Divine Love reach new pinnacles, suggesting that love in the Divine Will extends beyond human understanding. It is an eternal flame that warms not just the lover but all creation. This divine love is boundless, encompassing every creature and all of creation, urging believers to transcend personal love and embrace a universal compassion that mirrors God's infinite love for humanity.

Volumes 11-20 also emphasize the Divine Will's transformative power over human nature. Believers are called to allow the Divine Will to subsume their being wholly, purging every imperfection and aligning every thought, word, and deed with divine purposes. The transformational journey depicted in these volumes reinforces the belief that ultimate sanctity and divine union are achievable in this life.

These features, painted across ten volumes, construct an epic narrative that speaks directly to the hearts of Roman Catholics. Each volume acts as a beacon, guiding souls through the labyrinthine journey of faith, suffering, love, and divine union. The teachings are not to overwhelm but to inspire, shedding divine light on the path to living wholly in the Divine Will.

Thus, as one traverses the sacred passages of Volumes 11 through 20, the tapestry of divine revelation unfurls, revealing the sublime architecture of God's Will. Each thread is woven with intention, each color reflective of the boundless love and unending grace that God bestows upon humanity. These volumes are treasures of heavenly wisdom, urging all who read them to delve deeper into the Divine Will and to allow its transformative power to shine through every aspect of life.

Highlights From Volumes 21-29

In the resplendent chronicles of Volumes 21 through 29, a profound deepening of the Divine Will's mysteries unfolds, much like the unfurling petals of a celestial flower. These volumes, bathed in the ethereal light of divine wisdom, draw the soul ever closer to the ineffable Heart of Our Lord. Herein, the teachings transcend mere human understanding, weaving a tapestry that is at once both intricate and glorious, showcasing the boundless depth and breadth of God's plan for humanity.

Volume 21 commences with a divine illumination into the necessity of living entirely within the Divine Will. The secret to ultimate union with the Creator is revealed through the metaphor of the circle—a symbol of infinity, without beginning or end, much like the eternal nature of God's love for His creation. The call to dissolve personal will into the Divine Will is stark yet compelling, urging every soul to strive for a surrender that mirrors the humility of the Blessed Virgin.

As we proceed into Volume 22, the emphasis on the Divine Will as the source of all virtues becomes vivid. It articulates how, united with Divine Will, one's actions—even the simplest of gestures—transcend into acts of divine love and mercy. This transformative union turns daily routines into a sanctified rhythm of celestial harmony, a dance choreographed by the Divine Maestro.

The narrative of Volume 23 delves into the boundless mercy of God and the inexhaustible graces one receives when living in the Divine Will. The soul, described as a vessel, is continually filled and refilled by this divine outpouring until it overflows, spilling its heavenly contents into the world. These teachings encourage the faithful to become conduits of God's grace, spreading His loving presence wherever they tread.

Volume 24 illuminates the celestial aspect of the virtue of obedience, not as a mere duty but as a profound act of love. The pages recount Christ's own obedience unto death, urging the faithful to emulate this purity of intention. Such obedience in the Divine Will is portrayed as a golden thread that binds the human heart to the Sacred Heart of Jesus, creating an eternal bond grounded in divine fidelity.

The radiance of Volume 25 is found in its exposition of divine providence and the mysterious ways it orchestrates the events of human lives. It reassures the faithful that nothing is ever outside the watchful gaze of God. Every joy, every sorrow, every trial, is part of His magnificent tapestry, intricately woven with the golden threads of His Divine Will. Surrendering to this providence requires an abandonment that is both profound and liberating, releasing the soul from the shackles of fear and worry.

In Volume 26, the teachings soar to a sublime crescendo, revealing the unending exchange of love between the Creator and creation. This celestial dialogue is sustained by the Divine Will, akin to an eternal symphony where each note is an act of love. Here, the soul is invited to participate actively in this exchange, offering itself as a humble, yet essential, note in the divine composition.

With Volume 27, the focus shifts to the mystical union that the soul attains when fully subsumed in the Divine Will. This union is likened to a majestic marriage, wherein the soul becomes the bride of Christ, adorned by the virtues of faith, hope, and charity. This betrothal is not reserved for the saints and mystics alone but is offered to every soul willing to relinquish self-will in favor of divine love.

Volume 28 continues this theme, expounding on the role of suffering in the journey toward divine union. It portrays suffering not as a curse but as a sanctifying force that molds the soul into a perfect instrument of God's Will. By embracing sufferings willingly, the soul participates in Christ's redemptive passion, thereby contributing to the salvation of the world. It is a poignant reminder that through the thorns, one finds the rose of divine grace.

The last in this august series, Volume 29, is a crescendo of divine revelation, delving into the eschatological implications of living in the Divine Will. It speaks of a future where all creation will perfectly reflect the Divine Will, heralding an era of peace and unity. This prophetic vision serves both as a goal and a promise, urging the faithful to persevere in their journey, buoyed by the hope of this divine fulfillment.

Thus, these volumes collectively serve as a majestic guide, drawing the soul deeper into the divine mystery and closer to the eternal embrace of the Divine Will. In surrendering to this sacred call, one begins to live not merely as a creature but as a co-participant in the divine plan, reflecting the glory and splendor of God through every thought, word, and deed.

The salient lessons and revelations from these volumes powerfully underscore the transformative essence of the Divine Will. The teachings are a clarion call, urging the soul to rise from the mire of earthly concerns and soar toward the heavenly realms, carried aloft by the wings of divine wisdom and grace. Each word, each page, is imbued with the fragrance of celestial insight, inviting the faithful into the grand narrative of God's everlasting love.

By embracing these divine teachings, one embarks on a journey that transcends time and space, a pilgrimage toward a celestial union that is both the soul's origin and its ultimate destination. Submerged in the Divine Will, life is not merely lived; it is sanctified, elevated, and woven into the eternal story of divine love and grace, transforming the mundane into the miraculous.

The fruits of these teachings are manifold, offering a life replete with divine virtues, suffused with peace, and radiant with the light of God's presence. The soul, dedicated to living in the Divine Will, becomes a mirror reflecting the boundless love of the Creator, a vessel of His infinite mercy, and an instrument of His divine purpose. Thus, embracing the wisdom of Volumes 21 through 29 is not merely an act of faith but a transformative journey into the very heart of God.

Highlights From Volumes 30-36

In those revered tomes, Volumes 30 through 36 of the Book of Heaven, the profound tapestry of Divine Will is further unravelled. These later volumes, authored by the illustrious hand of Luisa Piccarreta under divine inspiration, offer paramount insights for those who seek to immerse themselves in the sacred doctrine of living in the Divine Will. Each page pulsates with celestial revelations, driving forward the tenets of a life entirely consecrated to God's Will.

Firstly, Volume 30 delivers an ardent call for mankind to embrace a perfect union with Divine Will. It is in this union that the soul finds its true genesis and ultimate purpose. Luisa elucidates the intricate dance between human will and Divine Will, illuminating how one's total abandonment to God's desire ushers in ineffable peace and heavenly felicity. The soul, she writes, becomes a mirror reflecting God's infinite love and wisdom upon the earth, an emissary of divine grace in a world much in need of light.

As we journey into Volume 31, we are met with a divine crescendo. Herein, the Lord unveils the eternal days of the Kingdom of Divine Will which have no night, for darkness is dispelled by the eternal light of God's presence. This metaphor speaks not just of a physical reality, but a spiritual one where sorrow and anguish are no more, replaced by the perpetual dawn of divine fulfillment. The celestial narrative accentuates that living in the Divine Will transforms every mundane act into an act of eternal worth, sanctified and magnified in the eyes of God.

Volume 32 delves deeper into the metaphysics of Divine Will, portraying a vivid picture of the soul that exists as an orb of divine light. This light, nourished by God Himself, spreads forth to touch all creation. It is in these profound revelations that Luisa speaks of a future era, a time when the Kingdom of Divine Will shall reign supreme. The soul, participating in such divine grandeur, serves as a beacon of hope to mankind, intricately woven into the divine fabric of salvation history.

The subsequent Volume 33 emphasizes the role of suffering and sacrifice, not as mere trials, but as divine instruments of sanctification. Luisa narrates that every pang of suffering, every cross borne with love, is transmuted into a powerful force of redemption for oneself and others. Such suffering, united with the passions of Christ, illuminates the path of divine will, making our earthly struggles a crucial component of divine providence.

When we arrive at Volume 34, we encounter the profound revelation of the Divine Will as the ultimate law governing the universe. The celestial symbolism employed by Luisa likens this law to a golden thread, binding together the cosmos in harmonious obedience to God's eternal plan. This divine orchestration is a testament to God's omniscience and omnipotence, inviting every soul to walk in perfect harmony with His will. It is a clarion call to recognize the omnipresence of God's design in both the grand and the minute facets of life.

Volume 35, with its poetic fervor, breathes life into the concept of divine love. Here, Luisa articulates that Divine Will is synonymous with divine love, both being inseparable attributes of God's infinite nature. The soul, in surrendering to Divine Will, is engulfed in this eternal love, becoming a vessel through which God's love flows freely. This divine love purifies, sanctifies, and elevates the soul to a state of sublime communion with the Creator, forging an indissoluble bond of divine intimacy.

Finally, Volume 36 culminates the celestial anthology with an awakening to the perpetual reality of living in Divine Will. It is a declaration of the soul's final homecoming, a return to the primordial state of grace as intended by God. This volume underscores the transformation that occurs when one lives in perfect accord with Divine Will—natural existence is elevated to supernatural realms, where every breath, thought, and action attains eternal significance. It is a promise of ultimate fulfillment and unending joy, a foretaste of the heavenly banquet.

Through these volumes, it becomes abundantly clear that to live in Divine Will is not merely an act of passive surrender but an active participation in God's eternal creative work. Each revelation laid down by Luisa is akin to a divine brushstroke painting the grand mural of redemption and sanctification, inviting every soul to become a co-creator with the Divine Master. The spiritual profundity encapsulated in these teachings beckons every faithful to partake in an intimate dance with the Divine, where every step resonates with the harmony of celestial music.

Volumes 30 through 36, therefore, serve as a crescendo of divine symphony, drawing the reader into deeper communion with the Divine Will. They are not merely texts to be read but divine script to be lived and incarnated in the soul of every believer. The essence herein lies not in mere comprehension but in the transformative experience of living wholly immersed in the Divine Will, thus fulfilling God's eternal plan for mankind.

Embedded within these sacred volumes is a timeless message that transcends earthly constraints, urging a return to a state of divine unity and harmony. Each soul is called to realize its potential as a bearer of divine light, participating in the sacred mission of salvation and sanctification. The road to divine will is paved with divine revelations, beckoning every faithful Roman Catholic to tread upon it with fervor, conviction, and unwavering faith.

Chapter 11: Major Principles Of The Divine Will

In the sacred realm of the Divine Will, one discovers the profound essence of living as God intended, where each soul is called to experience the seamless unity with Him. This spiritual journey beckons us to relinquish our own desires, embracing instead the boundless providence of the Creator. The core principles invite us to a deeper communion with the Father, promoting an existence where divine love, humility, and obedience reign supreme. It is not merely an adherence to commands, but a wholehearted participation in God's eternal plan, aligning our will with His. The teachings of Luisa Piccarreta reveal this divine invitation, urging the faithful to transform every act, breath, and heartbeat into an offering of love, thereby fostering a world permeated by His Holy Will. Through prayer, sacrifice, and continual surrender, believers become living reflections of divine grace, dwelling within the harmony of Heaven and Earth united.

Living In The Divine Will

The essence of "Living in the Divine Will" transcends human comprehension, for it immerses the soul into the very heartbeat of God, aligning every thought, word, and action with His eternal plan. To live in the Divine Will is not merely to do God's will, for men have strived towards this noble end since time immemorial. Rather, it is to live as though one was a transparent conduit of the Divine, where the soul's will is absorbed and governed wholly by God's will. This state can be considered the most august invitation extended to humanity, a divine partnership where the infinite and finite interlace, not in essence but in operation.

In this union, the soul becomes a mirror of divine attributes. Humility, patience, and charity are no longer pursued as distant virtues but become the natural breath of one's being. The words of Christ to Luisa Piccarreta aptly capture this transformation: "My daughter, as the soul lives in My Will, she accomplishes all acts and embraces all creatures. My Will is the veil that covers all acts of creatures, be they good or evil, so that the human acts, at their origins, are divine." Thus, the profound communion becomes evident, where human actions are sanctified and magnified by the divine intent.

To live in the Divine Will is to partake in a cosmic liturgy, a continuous act of divine worship that is not confined to the walls of a church or the hours of prayer. Every mundane task, every fleeting thought, becomes a sanctuary where grace flows unimpeded. The soul, liberated from the shackles of self-will, rests in perpetual adoration and submission. It is akin to the angels, whose very existence is a pure act of worship.

The life in the Divine Will brings forth an unparalleled intimacy with the Holy Trinity. The soul, dwelling in the Divine Will, finds itself nestled in the love of the Father, the grace of the Son, and the sanctifying action of the Holy Spirit. This triune presence becomes as real and palpable as the air we breathe, an interior life rich with divine dialogues and celestial inspirations.

Living in the Divine Will is also a return to the primordial peace enjoyed by Adam and Eve in the Garden of Eden before the fall. The historical wound of original sin and its consequences are transcended. The soul, clothed anew with divine grace, walks in the simplicity and innocence of an unfallen state, resonating with the harmony of creation. As such, the soul contributes to the reintegration of all things in Christ, hastening the coming of the Kingdom.

Yet, this calling is not without its trials and tribulations. The process of annihilating self-will and surrendering wholly to Divine Will is often accompanied by profound interior struggles. The soul must grapple with its attachments, ego, and the lure of worldly desires. It is a crucible where the dross of human imperfection is burned away to reveal the gold of divine likeness. Through prayer, sacramental life, and constant yearning for divine union, the soul perseveres, fortified by the grace of God.

This path, as revealed to Luisa Piccarreta, is not an isolated journey but a communal one. It calls the faithful to be ambassadors of divine light in a world shrouded in darkness. By living in the Divine Will, one becomes a beacon of hope and a channel of God's mercy to all. Communities and parishes can be transformed into lively expressions of God's kingdom, fostering unity, love, and charity.

Practicing the teachings of the Divine Will often starts with small, deliberate acts of surrender. Simple prayers like "Fiat" (let it be done) become the soul's constant refrain. This continuous act of abandonment, repeated in every moment, helps to cultivate an attitude of trust and dependence on God. Over time, this practice becomes second nature, and the soul naturally tends towards seeking and embracing God's will in all things.

The fruits of living in the Divine Will are manifold. Peace, joy, and a profound sense of purpose permeate the soul. There is a newfound freedom from the anxieties and fears that plague the human condition. Relationships are healed and deepened, as the soul sees Christ in every person. The entire being becomes a testament to the power and love of God, effortlessly drawing others towards the light of Christ.

In conclusion, living in the Divine Will is the ultimate fulfillment of Christ's prayer, "Thy kingdom come, Thy will be done on earth as it is in heaven." It is a call to restoration, to return to the heart of the Father, and to live as true children of God. As we embrace this divine calling, our lives become a symphony of grace, an unceasing hymn of glory to the Creator. The journey may be arduous, but the reward is eternal: union with the Divine Will and participation in the very life of God. In this, we find our true meaning and our ultimate destiny.

Practicing The Teachings

The journey towards practicing the teachings of the Divine Will requires an immersion into the fountain of celestial wisdom contained within the "Book of Heaven." It is an unwavering plunge into the abyss of divine love, crafted meticulously by the hand of our Creator Himself. As Roman Catholics committed to these teachings, one must take on the mantle of humility and faith, seeing everyday moments as opportunities for divine transformation.

First and foremost, understanding the Divine Will is not merely an intellectual endeavor but a lived reality. There needeth be a sincere dedication to continuous prayer, reflecting the heart and soul's ardent desire to align with God's ultimate plan. Our daily offerings should be intertwined with our labor and leisure, creating a tapestry of worship that honors the Divine Will in every facet of life.

The teachings of the Book of Heaven call us to an intimate union with the Creator, beyond the rudiments of perfunctory observances. It beckons a transformation wherein every action, no matter how mundane, is sanctified and aligned with the divine purpose. This alignment manifests through acts of virtue, where love, patience, humility, and obedience harmonize with God's Will, fostering communal and individual sanctity.

Observance of the Divine Will also mandates a keen awareness of unceasing divine presence, a spiritual vigilantism that keeps one attuned to God's subtle whispers. This vigilantism is nurtured through meditative contemplation on the sacred texts, allowing the words to penetrate deep into the heart, much like seeds sown into fertile soil, growing into a fruitful harvest of spiritual fortitude.

In practical life, the faithful adherent must strive to practice empathy and charity, reflecting Christ's commandment of loving one's neighbor. Acts of kindness and mercy, done for the glory of God, become pathways through which the Divine Will operates, enriching both the giver and the recipient. Such practices are not mere acts of human goodwill; they are embodiments of divine love pouring forth from those who live in unity with God's Will.

Moreover, the setting of examples is paramount. To practice the teachings is to become a living gospel, an embodiment of divine truth, prompting others to look towards the higher realm of divine purpose. This is achieved through steadfastness in trials and unwavering faith amidst tribulations, portraying the very essence of divine trust and surrender.

Collective worship and community life also play a crucial role. Engaging in communal prayers, Eucharistic adoration, and regular participation in the sacraments enriches one's journey in practicing the Divine Will. The community, as a body of Christ, provides support, encouragement, and accountability, reinforcing the values and teachings in everyday life.

In this pursuit, one must also embrace silence and solitude, allowing times of reflection to deepen one's relationship with God. Silence is the sacred space where God speaks to the soul, and solitude the fertile ground where His Will is discerned and embraced. Through such practices, the faithful can better understand their own divine vocations and the specific roles they play in the grand tapestry of God's plan.

It is also vital to be ardent students of the Book of Heaven, continually delving into its volumes. Regular study groups, discussions, and personal reflections on these texts fortify the spiritual journey, providing fresh insights and understanding into the depths of Divine Will. In such engagements, the teachings become more than words on a page; they are transformed into living principles guiding daily actions.

Forging ahead, the practice of the Divine Will demands constancy and endurance. It is a clarion call to rise above fleeting worldly concerns and to place undivided trust in God's Providence. This entails an unrelenting commitment to discipleship, willingly embracing sacrificial love and carrying the cross in union with Christ.

Furthermore, it is essential to cultivate a spirit of gratitude, recognizing the manifold graces and blessings bestowed upon us. A grateful heart is a heart attuned to the Divine Will, seeing every situation, even adversities, as expressions of God's loving care. Gratitude nurtures joy and contentment, essential virtues for anyone on this divine journey.

In summation, practicing the teachings of the Divine Will is an immersive, all-encompassing endeavor that integrates the celestial with the mundane. It beckons the faithful to transcend ordinary existence, living each day with a heightened awareness of God's omnipresence and omnipotence. By embracing prayer, communal support, contemplation, and continuous study, Roman Catholics can truly live out the Divine Will, becoming beacons of God's love and conveyors of His divine plan.

Chapter 12: Comparative Study With Other Private Revelations

Verily, when we embark upon a comparative study of the Divine Will revelations given unto Luisa Piccarreta with those bestowed upon Saint Faustina and through the Marian apparitions, an illustrious tapestry of divine intent reveals itself. These sacrosanct communications, each unique yet symphonious with the sacred tradition of Holy Mother Church, elucidate and affirm the unchanging love and will of the Almighty. Within the pages of Luisa's Book of Heaven, one is beckoned to fathom the profundities of living in the Divine Will, a calling unparalleled yet complementing the merciful overtures recorded in Saint Faustina's Diary. The Marian apparitions, laden with celestial wisdom, further echo this divine cadence, summoning humanity towards an existence deeply interwoven with God's will. Through this synthesis, the Divine Will movement emerges not as an isolated phenomenon but as a luminous thread woven through the broad canvas of divine disclosures, rendering the hem of heaven's garment visible upon earth.

St. Faustina's Diary

Within the shining constellation of private revelations that illuminate the firmament of the Church's spiritual heritage, St. Faustina's Diary bears a unique radiance. The Divine Mercy revelations conferred upon St. Maria Faustina Kowalska, a humble Polish nun, evoke a compelling narrative that intertwines seamlessly with the broader thematic tapestry of Luisa Piccarreta's Book of Heaven. We endeavor here, not to pluck apart their distinct celestial flowers but to weave their fragrances into a unified bouquet, revealing how each, in its own exceptional manner, calls the faithful to a deeper immersion into God's unfathomable Will.

St. Faustina's Diary, formally titled "Divine Mercy in My Soul," reveals profound treasures wherein Jesus speaks of His boundless mercy, inviting souls to trust in Him. The pages of her diary, rich with mystical experiences and Christ's direct communications, hold up a mirror to the teachings found within the Book of Heaven. Indeed, both speak of divine love that goes beyond the immediate grasp of human comprehension, yet becomes a palpable reality through living in union with God's Will.

Akin to the revelations bestowed upon Luisa Piccarreta, St. Faustina's experiences provide a continuous thread that demonstrates the depths of divine intimacy available to those fervent in prayer and surrender. While the Book of Heaven articulates a more expansive blueprint of living in the Divine Will as infused into daily existence, Faustina's revelations emphasize the fountain of mercy flowing from Jesus' Sacred Heart. Both, however, beckon the faithful toward a sanctified existence steeped in divine grace.

Forsooth, the echoes of Christ's exhortations in St. Faustina's Diary resonate harmoniously with the core themes in Piccarreta's writings. Jesus' pleas for trust and His disclosures about the ocean of mercy He wishes to pour out upon humanity complement the dialogue on divine love found in the Book of Heaven. Where Faustina is called as an "Apostle of Divine Mercy," Luisa is revealed as "The Little Daughter of the Divine Will," each title underscoring a unique mission yet dwelling in the unity of divine purpose.

The intriguing aspect lies in the manner these two women received and recorded their communications from Jesus. Faustina's path was marked by dialogues infused with poetic imagery and visions, often centered around the Divine Mercy image and the Chaplet. Conversely, Piccarreta's spiritual journey is meticulously cataloged in the extensive volumes of the Book of Heaven, articulating the teachings on living continuously in the Divine Will with a clarity that fortifies the Church's doctrinal understandings.

It can be observed that St. Faustina's Diary emphasizes a heart-to-heart encounter with Christ, urging the devotee to trust in His mercy, while the Book of Heaven delves into a more intellectual appreciation of divine truths. This dichotomy, however, still leads to one singular path of love and surrender. In both their writings, the mercy and will of God are portrayed not as abstract theological concepts but as lived experiences deeply accessible through prayer and devotion.

Furthermore, the emphasis on divine timing and God's receptivity in human affairs come to the fore in both mystics' revelations. St. Faustina's encounters often highlight the urgent call for mercy in anticipation of the final judgment, whilst Luisa's volumes stress the ultimate restoration of God's Kingdom on Earth as it is in Heaven. Both paths reflect an eschatological dimension where human cooperation with divine grace hastens the fulfillment of God's salvific plan.

Art thou in doubt of the connection, consider the intricate harmony in their respective messages. Faustina's vision of the Divine Mercy Chaplet as a means of imploring God's mercy intersects effortlessly with Luisa's teachings on living in the Divine Will—which in itself is a continuous act of invoking God's mercy through one's life. Indeed, each Chaplet bead lifted in prayer joins its essence with the life lived in consonance with the Divine Will as elucidated by Piccarreta.

A further reflection affirms this cosmic symphony, embodied in their spiritual directives which call for trust and surrender. As Jesus instructed Faustina— "Jesus, I trust in You,"—we find resonance in Luisa's constant theme of surrender to the Divine Will— "Fiat!" The foundation of both their teachings lies in the abandonment to divine providence, a surrender that unites the soul more profoundly with the heart of Christ than any rational endeavor could attempt.

Assuredly, the fruits born from these two spiritual trees bear witness to the unity of their divine inspirations. Devotions to the Divine Mercy have flourished, leading countless souls to the sacraments and a profound trust in God's love. Similarly, those who practice living in the Divine Will recount transformative experiences that deepen their fidelity to Christ and His Church. Their shared emphasis on confession and Eucharistic devotion charts a path readily accessible to all faithful, guiding them through the narrow gate to the immense Kingdom of God.

Let us also acknowledge the mystical sufferings endured by both saints in service of divine union. St. Faustina's acceptance of physical and spiritual trials mirrors Luisa's profound participation in the Passion of Christ. These chosen souls, through their sufferings, epitomize the call to co-suffer with Christ, a testament to their ultimate trust and submission to His Holy Will.

Bringing to light their complementary revelations, we are given a holistic framework on the divine qualities of mercy and the Will that guide our salvation history. St. Faustina's heartfelt revelations encapsulate the mercy that flows directly from God's heart, creating a gateway through which souls may enter the sanctum of His love. Piccarreta's extensive dialogues unfold the edifice of living perpetually in divine intimacy, directed by the Holy Spirit, broadening the panorama viewed through Faustina's lens.

In considering the immense spiritual wealth enshrined within St. Faustina's Diary and Luisa Piccarreta's Book of Heaven, it becomes indubitably clear that the faithful are invited into an ever-deepening relationship with God. St. Faustina's message, channeled through the Divine Mercy image and devotion, complements Luisa's teachings on the perennial embrace of God's Will, thus furnishing a comprehensive itinerary for sanctification.

In conclusion, St. Faustina's Diary and Luisa Piccarreta's Book of Heaven, though distinct in their particulars, form a harmonious concord, each enriching the other. The apostolic zeal for divine mercy dovetails seamlessly with living in God's Will, ultimately drawing the tapestry of salvation tighter. In this divine interplay, one perceives the continuity of God's revelations, inviting His faithful into the depths of His ineffable mercy and Will, thus rendering a compelling narrative that beckons all to lose themselves in the infinite love of our Creator.

The Marian Apparitions

Upon the vast tapestry of divine revelations granted to humanity, the Marian Apparitions occupy a perennial and illustrious thread. The Mother of God, in her manifold visitations to the children of men, has heralded messages of grace, repentance, and divine love, which remain indelibly etched upon the Christian conscience. From the verdant meadows of Lourdes to the sunlit hills of Fatima, the Blessed Virgin has adorned the pages of sacred history with celestial encounters that echo the immutable truths of Heaven.

Each apparition unfolds amidst a unique backdrop, enshrouded in divine mystery, yet resplendent with profound consistency. For instance, in the hallowed grotto of Lourdes in 1858, the Immaculate Conception presented herself to the humble Bernadette Soubirous, proclaiming the necessity of prayer and penance. Similarly, in Fatima in 1917, the Holy Virgin appeared to three shepherd children, imparting secrets that unveiled both the horrors of war and the hope of peace rooted in devout consecration to her Immaculate Heart.

The apparitions are marked not only by their consistent themes of repentance and fidelity but also by the tangible manifestations of divine will and miraculous interventions. At Guadaloupe in 1531, the tilma of Saint Juan Diego became an enduring testament to the Blessed Virgin's presence, enshrining her image as a perpetual invitation to conversion. Likewise, at Fatima, the Miracle of the Sun, witnessed by tens of thousands, stands as a resounding affirmation of the celestial message.

In pondering these divine visitations, one discerns an intricate interplay between the Marian messages and the broader corpus of Catholic revelation. Each apparition acts as both a reaffirmation and a unique exposition of the divine will, harmonizing seamlessly with the teachings expounded in the Book of Heaven. Just as the Blessed Mother calls the faithful to attune their lives to divine love, so too does the Divine Will Movement exhort believers to live in a state of continual communion with God.

Indeed, the Marian Apparitions converge with Luisa Piccarreta's revelations, presenting a unified front of divine exhortation. Both the Blessed Mother's apparitions and Luisa's writings bespeak a profound unity of purpose: to draw humanity into a deeper relationship with the divine. This can be seen in Mary's messages directing the faithful toward the Sacraments and the life of virtue, mirroring the Divine Will's call for a life immersed in God's presence.

Furthermore, the thematic overlap is profound. Consider Fatima's urgency for reparation and consecration to the Immaculate Heart. This call resonates with Luisa Piccarreta's teachings on living in the Divine Will, which emphasizes reparation for sin and the fulfillment of God's desires as central tenets. Thus, the Marian apparitions serve not only as prophetic utterances but as luminous guides that point to the same divine truth expounded within the Book of Heaven.

Moreover, these heavenly encounters possess an eschatological dimension, forecasting the ultimate triumph of divine love and justice. For instance, the apparition at La Salette foretells chastisements for unrepented sin, while also offering a vision of eventual peace and renewal. Likewise, the messages received by Luisa paint a landscape wherein the Divine Will shall reign supreme, bringing about a new era of holiness and divine intimacy.

Another significant aspect is the role of human intermediaries within both realms of revelation. The seers of the Marian apparitions, often humble and meek, resemble Luisa Piccarreta in their simplicity and obedience. Their lives serve as exemplars of docility to divine promptings, demonstrating that God chooses the lowly to confound the wise. The spiritual journeys of these privileged souls become a living testament to the transformative power of divine grace.

It is imperative to recognize that the fruit of these apparitions, much like the teachings of the Divine Will Movement, extends beyond the recipients themselves to the broader ecclesial community. Pilgrims flock to Marian shrines, seeking solace and conversion, much as readers of the Book of Heaven find nourishment and inspiration in its pages. Both serve to reinvigorate the spiritual life of the faithful, fostering communal and individual sanctification.

Additionally, the Marian apparitions often bear ecclesiastical approval, signifying their consonance with sacred tradition and magisterial teaching. This acceptance underscores the harmony between these private revelations and the Church's doctrinal corpus. Similarly, the Divine Will Movement, though scrutinized and sometimes misunderstood, gradually garners ecclesiastic support, echoing the Church's cautious but affirming stance towards Marian apparitions.

The significance of these Marian visitations cannot be fully grasped without acknowledging their role in spiritual warfare. Many apparitions occur during tumultuous periods, offering consolation amid societal upheaval. In this light, the messages of the Divine Will provide believers with the spiritual armor necessary to navigate the vicissitudes of modern life, promising victory through total surrender to God's will.

To encapsulate the essence of the Marian apparitions within the comprehensive study of private revelations, one must recognize their unparalleled contribution to the continuum of divine instruction. They are not relics of a bygone era but living dialogues between Heaven and Earth, ever-relevant and effulgent with divine wisdom. In them, we glimpse the contours of divine mercy and the ardent call to holiness echoed through the perennial voice of the Mother of God.

The Marian apparitions, therefore, stand as celestial beacons, illuminating the path towards a fuller understanding and living out of the Divine Will. They are testimonies to God's unceasing dialogue with humanity, urging souls towards the eternal embrace of divine love, a goal most profoundly elucidated through the Divine Will teachings. Hence, in drawing connections between Marian revelations and the insights offered to Luisa Piccarreta, we uncover a divine symphony of messages, all converging towards the singular aim of leading souls to the ultimate fulfillment of God's eternal plan.

Chapter 13: Examining Criticisms And Misunderstandings

Amidst the sacred tomes and divine revelations bestowed upon the virgin soul of Luisa Piccarreta, critiques arise like shadows in the glorious dawn. Misunderstandings, oft borne of ignorance or fear, seek to mar the luminous truth of the Divine Will Movement. Some dissenters, tethered to worldly interpretations, mistake the sanctity of these writings. They argue, questioning the alignment of the Book of Heaven with Sacred Tradition, even though the Church's Magisterium regards these revelations with reverence. Others, puzzled by the profound notion of living in the Divine Will, err in dismissing it as impractical. Yet, by cherishing these heavenly insights, one finds harmony with the core teachings of Holy Mother Church, wherein the Divine Will is neither new nor foreign, but eternal. Thus, each criticism, when examined with a discerning heart and open mind, unravels, leaving the Divine Will Movement pristine and resplendent, a testament to God's omnipotent plan.

Common Misconceptions

In the celestial quest to commune with God's Divine Will, one encounters various misconceptions that shadow the luminous truths held within the Book of Heaven. These misunderstandings, often borne of superficial examination or predisposed skepticism, must be steadfastly dispelled.

Foremost among these is the notion that the teachings of Luisa Piccarreta diverge from established Church doctrine. Such an assertion unravels with meticulous study; examination discloses the profound harmony between Luisa's revelations and the magisterial teachings of Holy Mother Church. Indeed, the revelations strictly adhere to the traditions of the saints and the ecclesiastical mandates, forming a magnificent tapestry that reflects the divine orthodoxy.

Another misconception to address pertains to the perceived exclusivity of the Divine Will. Critics might argue that these revelations assert a nouvelle and elitist form of spirituality, transcending the common experience of the laity. Yet, this accusation falters under scrutiny. The Book of Heaven extends not an invitation to the elect few but an allencompassing call to all souls thirsting for divine intimacy. The teachings of Luisa offer a universal path designed to bridge all faithful souls with the divine intention, allowing them to partake in the Divine Will.

Equally insidious is the misunderstanding that the Divine Will Movement espouses a passive spirituality, suggesting that adherents neglect works of mercy and active virtue. Quite oppositely, the movement invigorates the practitioner to engage more fervently in Christ-like acts of charity and love. Living in the Divine Will impels one's actions to be wholly transformed, animated by divine grace, thereby enhancing the virtue of every act and embedding it in the eternal will of God.

The accusers also err when they lament an ostensible obsolescence of personal initiative. They misconstrue the surrender to God's Will as a surrender of human agency. This perception could not be further from the truth. Embracing the Divine Will requires a profound act of human will—a conscious and deliberate choice to align one's desires with the divine. This alignment does not nullify personal initiative but rather sanctifies it, imbuing human actions with eternal significance.

Another errant belief suggests that the Book of Heaven is merely a collection of pious reflections, rather than divinely inspired revelation. To consign these luminous writings to mere devotional literature reduces their transcendent revelations to the mundane. The expository splendor with which Luisa Piccarreta conveys God's messages bears the mark of divine origin, touching theological depths and spiritual heights that beckon serious contemplation and reverence. The Church's careful and ongoing examination of Luisa's writings further underscores their divine provenance.

It is also worth noting the concern regarding the mystical nature of Luisa's experiences. Some question the authenticity of her mysticism, mistaking her profound spiritual encounters for mere hallucinations or fabrications. To dismiss her experiences in such a manner is to overlook the rigorous discernment processes conducted by the Church. Luisa's spirituality, marked by her mystical union with Christ and profound humility, aligns with the spiritual experiences of other renowned mystics recognized by the Church.

Moreover, some detractors argue that the Divine Will teachings render other Christian practices and devotions obsolete. They fear that an emphasis on the Divine Will diminishes the value of traditional prayers, sacraments, and devotions. This misconception is a distortion of the teachings. The Divine Will does not replace, but rather, enriches these practices. When living in the Divine Will, every prayer, every sacramental act is elevated, infused with a deeper, divine significance.

Furthermore, some raise concerns about the language and symbolic references used in Luisa's writings, which at times may appear esoteric or difficult to interpret. This complexity, however, is not a barrier but an invitation to delve deeper into the mysteries of God. Spiritual language often transcends ordinary human speech, inviting believers to engage with the texts meditatively and prayerfully, thereby opening themselves to greater understanding through divine illumination.

Some also suspect that the teachings of the Book of Heaven promote an overemphasis on suffering, misconstruing the acceptance of divine suffering as a call to seek pain for its own sake. This is a misunderstanding of the profound spiritual reality Luisa presents. The teachings underscore the redemptive value of suffering when united with Christ's Passion. Far from a morbid fascination, this portrays a pathway to deep union with Christ, transforming suffering into a powerful act of love and participation in redemption.

Lastly, some skeptics argue that the devotion to the Divine Will is a distraction from the centrality of the Gospel and the core tenets of the Catholic faith. They perceive it as an extraneous addition rather than an integral element. However, when properly understood, the Divine Will teachings illuminate the very essence of the Gospel. They call believers to live out the fullness of Christ's prayer to His Father: "Thy will be done on earth as it is in heaven." This is not a departure from the faith but a fulfillment of its deepest call.

Indeed, the persistence of these misconceptions draws attention to the need for ongoing education and catechesis. Scholars and theologians must continue to elucidate the profound theological and spiritual insights contained within Luisa Piccarreta's writings. Only through dedicated study and open-hearted engagement can these misunderstandings be addressed and the true beauty of the Divine Will be fully appreciated.

By dismantling these misconceptions, we clear the path for a more profound and transformative engagement with the Divine Will. We open ourselves to a spirituality that does not substitute but elevates our faith, that does not confine but frees us to live more fully in the presence of God. Let us journey forward, unencumbered by misunderstanding, towards the radiant truth of living in the Divine Will.

The Church's Stance

In a world beset by myriad voices clamoring for attention, the Church remains the steadfast custodian of Divine truth, guiding the faithful through the labyrinth of temporal existence. The revelations given to Luisa Piccarreta and inscribed within "The Book of Heaven" have not been exempt from scrutiny, raised eyebrows, and the probing inquiries of both the curious and the skeptical. Indeed, it is thus the Church must exercise her divine mandate to discern, validate, and uphold teachings that further the sanctification of her flock.

The Magisterium, endowed with the solemn duty of maintaining doctrinal integrity, approaches private revelations with a balance of prudence and receptivity. Critical in the Church's discernment process is whether such revelations align harmoniously with Sacred Scripture and Tradition. To this end, myriad theologians and clerics have undertaken rigorous examination of Piccarreta's writings, mindful of St. Paul's exhortation to "test everything; hold fast what is good."

Through arduous investigation, several salient points emerge that elucidate the Church's stance on the Divine Will Movement. Firstly, the Church looks favorably upon the unshakable orthodoxy manifest within "The Book of Heaven." Piccarreta's revelations do not introduce novel doctrines but rather expand upon established theological principles. They bid the believer to unite one's own will with the Divine Will, an aspiration deeply rooted in the annals of Catholic mysticism and the pursuit of sanctity. Her writings echo, rather than detract from, scions of faith such as St. Teresa of Avila and St. John of the Cross.

Moreover, theological veneration is afforded to the impeccably Trinitarian nature of the revelations. The Divine Will, as articulated by Piccarreta, underscores the infinite confluence and communal love of the Father, Son, and Holy Spirit. Such teachings grace the faithful with a profound comprehension of intimate union with the Divine, in a manner congruent with the Church's Trinitarian dogma.

On another count, the notable ecclesiastical approbations granted to Piccarreta's cause offer further testament to the Church's affirmation. The diocesan process for her beatification commenced in 1994, indicating recognition of her virtuous life and the spiritual merit of her writings. Cardinal-former archbishop of Trani-Barletta-Bisceglie, Bishop Giovanni Battista Pichierri, a staunch supporter, acknowledged the theological profundity and spiritual fecundity of the Divine Will teachings. Such endorsements signal to the faithful that her writings bear substantial devotional and doctrinal value.

However, mindful of the diverse reception among the faithful, the Church treads with deliberate caution, wary of speculative fervor that might arise. The Vatican has yet to issue a definitive declaration, exercising its duty with pastoral sensitivity and theological rigor. Were such revelations to ignite misguided zeal or doctrinal confusion, the Church would act to mitigate such risks. This measured prudence should be interpreted not as an indictment but as an embodiment of maternal care, guiding the faithful as they navigate the intricacies of ecclesiastical discernment.

Furthermore, the writings of Luisa Piccarreta have been subject to theological scrutiny to ensure they do not conflict with the deposit of faith. Scholars wielding the tools of exegesis and historical theology examine the nuanced dimensions of her teachings. Their analyses aim to underscore that the Divine Will Movement is not a departure from, but an enrichment of, traditional Catholic spirituality. Hence, the Church's stance embodies a dynamic interplay of doctrinal fidelity and pastoral vigilance.

The Church extends an invitation to all to engage with Piccarreta's revelations with a discerning heart. Those who have tread the path illuminated by the Divine Will Movement attest to its transformative efficacy, their lives replete with newfound peace, purpose, and divine intimacy.

Under the watchful gaze of the Church, these experiences serve as potent testimonies of the fruitfulness of Piccarreta's writings. The Divine Will beckons the faithful toward a more profound communion with God, therein lies its sacred allure and divine promise.

In conclusion, the Church's stance on "The Book of Heaven" and the Divine Will Movement is emblematic of her timeless mission – to lead souls closer to the heart of the Divine. The ecclesiastical approbation, theological scrutiny, and pastoral guidance provided thus far point toward a revered treasure trove within the confines of these revelations. The faithful are encouraged to immerse themselves with a spirit of discernment and to journey ever deeper into the mystery of God's Divine Will.

Chapter 14: The Merging Of Divine Will And Sacred Tradition

As dawn melds with morning's splendor, so too has the sacred union of Divine Will and Sacred Tradition dawned upon the horizon of our spiritual journey. In an orchestrated symphony, the revelations entrusted to Luisa Piccarreta echo the timeless rhythms of Holy Scripture and the sagacious teachings handed down by the saints. This celestial confluence exemplifies not mere coincidence but the divine choreography of Providence, weaving Old and New, celestial and terrestrial, into an indissoluble tapestry. St. Augustine himself might marvel at such a harmonious convergence where the whispers of ancient faith blend with the proclamations heralded by modern visionaries. This sublime merging is not a departure from tradition but rather its exaltation, lifting the faithful to unprecedented heights of spiritual intimacy and understanding. Thus, the Divine Will manifests as both the root and the fruit—fortified by tradition, nourished by revelation, and flowering into a renewed promise of divine intimacy and eternal truth.

Deepening Understanding

In the sacred convergence of Divine Will and Sacred Tradition, one finds a profound tapestry woven from threads of celestial guidance and ecclesiastical wisdom. Embracing this union calls for an enlightened heart, one set on discerning the whispers of the Divine through the lens of venerable teachings handed down through the ages. It is the grand journey of the soul, venturing into the vast expanse where the Infinite stoops to touch the finite, where God's eternal plan and human history intertwine in a dance of grace and obedience.

The Book of Heaven, a treasury of divine revelations entrusted to Luisa Piccarreta, unfolds the magnificence of the Divine Will, calling the faithful to a deeper contemplation of God's mysteries. To comprehend the magnitude of these revelations and their alignment with Sacred Tradition, we must cultivate an intricate understanding that surpasses mere intellectual acceptance. This understanding beckons us to experience and live the teachings, immersing our very being in the essence of God's will.

Contemplating the profound mystery of Divine Will, one mustn't overlook the rich soil of Sacred Tradition in which it is grounded. This tradition, flourishing under the guardianship of the Church, provides the stable framework within which the revelations to Luisa find their home.

Reflect upon the wisdom of the Church Fathers, the doctrinal declarations, and the sacraments, all of which stand as pillars of our faith, ensuring that new revelations align with eternal truths. This is not a mere coincidence but a testament to the consistency of God's message across the ages.

Understanding the Divine Will requires an acceptance of not only the magnificence of God's sovereign plan but also the humility to abide by His commands. Luisa Piccarreta's journey is illustrative of this. Her extraordinary revelations often remind us of our need to be docile instruments in God's hands, facilitating the merging of our will with His. This profound harmonization is nothing short of transformative, beckoning us to renounce our temporal inclinations in favor of an eternal perspective.

To deepen our understanding, we must engage with Scriptural exegesis, theological reflections, and the lyrical expressions of mystics throughout church history. The Sacred Scriptures, replete with divine wisdom, illuminate the Divine Will, while the theological musings of scholars provide a structured comprehension of these holy texts. The writings of saints and mystics, marked by poetic fervor, add a layer of experiential knowledge, fostering a holistic grasp of God's designs.

As one sifts through the rich heritage of the Church, it becomes apparent that the Divine Will reverberates through the ages, hinting at an eternal harmony between heaven and earth. The lives of the saints offer luminous examples of this harmony. Saint Theresa's spiritual aspirations and Saint Francis's simplicity underscore the beautiful synchronicity between personal sanctity and Divine Will. Their lives, steeped in obedience and profound love, serve as beacons, guiding the faithful towards the ultimate fusion with God's desires.

The complexities of fully grasping the Divine Will might seem daunting, but the Holy Spirit, our Counselor, aids us in this endeavor. The Spirit's guidance leads us to discernment, encouraging us to see beyond the apparent and to recognize the divine orchestration in our lives. This divine assistance ensures that our deepening understanding is not merely an intellectual pursuit but an incarnational reality, where the Word made flesh dwells amongst us and in us.

Reflecting on the dogmas and doctrines that underpin our faith reveals the deep roots of the Divine Will in Sacred Tradition. Everything from the Immaculate Conception to the Assumption of Mary, from the Incarnation to the Eucharistic presence, speaks of God's will intertwining with human history. Indeed, the celebration of the liturgy itself manifests our participation in the Divine Will, a cosmic liturgy that connects heaven and earth in an eternal hymn of praise and thanksgiving.

Moreover, the teachings encapsulated in the Catechism and the writings of the Magisterium provide invaluable resources for our understanding. They offer clarity and guardrails, ensuring that our exploration of the Divine Will remains within the bounds of orthodox faith. The Magisterium's role is indispensable in affirming the veracity of revelations and integrating them into the life of the Church, thus ensuring continuity and fidelity to the Apostolic Tradition.

The journey towards a deeper understanding demands a heart free from attachment, open to divine grace and transformed by sacramental life. The sacraments, as channels of sanctifying grace, nourish our souls, equipping us to embrace God's will with steadfast courage. The Eucharist, in particular, is the zenith of divine intimacy, where we are united with Christ and, through Him, with the Divine Will. Frequent participation in the sacraments anchors our faith, fortifies our resolve and lights our path toward living in the Divine Will.

A deepened understanding requires dialoguing with God through prayer and meditation. This sacred conversation enlightens our minds and inflames our hearts, drawing us ever closer to His will. Engaging with the writings of Luisa Piccarreta through prayerful reading allows the Holy Spirit to illuminate our understanding, revealing the depths of God's love and His divine intentions for humanity. Through such prayer, we can steadily progress on the path laid out by Divine Providence.

In summation, the merging of Divine Will and Sacred Tradition is an invitation to a spiritual pilgrimage wherein one's understanding is continuously deepened. This merging isn't an academic exercise but a living reality, a dynamic interplay between divine revelation and the Church's enduring wisdom. By embracing this union, we not only enrich our faith but also partake in the divine life, becoming co-operators in God's grand design. In this sacred journey, faith and reason, heart and mind, tradition and revelation converge, guiding us into the fullness of truth and the immeasurable depths of God's eternal will.

Historical Cases

In the annals of Christendom, historical cases reveal a delicate interplay between Divine Will and Sacred Tradition, wherein Heaven's mandates both harmonize with and challenge the temporal edicts of the Church. Through the lens of time, we discern the complex tapestry of Divine Will interwoven with sacred traditions, illustrating how Heavenly revelations have long sought to enrich, not supplant, the fabric of established Church teachings. In examining these historical instances, we strengthen the argument that the revelations to Luisa Piccarreta have a venerable precedent and elucidate the Divine Will's symbiotic relationship with Sacred Tradition.

Consider the revelations to Saint Francis of Assisi, whose divine mission to live a life of apostolic poverty was initially met with skepticism by Church authorities. Despite the initial resistance, Saint Francis's unwavering commitment softened hearts, leading to the eventual papal endorsement of the Franciscan Rule. This not only reinforced the sanctity of his divine calling but also illustrated how new revelations can indeed deepen the Church's spiritual heritage. Even so, Francis's experiences forged a path for later revelations, such as those given to Luisa Piccarreta, as they too found a place within the ecclesiastical bosom.

Equally compelling are the cases of the Marian apparitions, specifically those at Lourdes and Fatima. Here, the Mother of God imparted messages of penance, prayer, and conversion, principles always cherished within the Church yet often needing revival through divine reinforcement. The rigor with which the Church scrutinized these apparitions, eventually recognizing their authenticity, parallels the ongoing discernment surrounding the works of Luisa Piccarreta. Just as the Marian messages invigorated the faithful and aligned with longstanding devotions, so do the teachings on living in the Divine Will aspire to renew and unify the Church's spiritual endeavors.

The mystical revelations to Saint Teresa of Ávila further elucidate how personal divine communications can both align with and enhance Church doctrine. As a Carmelite reformer and Doctor of the Church, Teresa's visions and spiritual insights did not veer from the bedrock of Sacred Tradition; rather, they illuminated the path to an enhanced spiritual life, inviting the devout into a deeper, more intimate communion with God. Such historical precedents resonate profoundly when considering Luisa Piccarreta's experiences, as both beckon the faithful to embrace God's will more completely.

Saint John of the Cross, a contemporary of Saint Teresa and another mystic whose insights were steeped in profound spiritual depth, also faced initial misunderstandings. His expositions on the 'Dark Night of the Soul' grappled with the intricacies of spiritual purification and union with God, concepts that the Church eventually recognized as transformative. Historically, his teachings, initially controversial, are now celebrated for their deep alignment with Church doctrine, providing a clear example of how divine revelations can face initial opposition but eventually bolster Sacred Tradition.

One must not overlook the cases within the Eastern Orthodoxy, where saints such as Sergius of Radonezh and Seraphim of Sarov received divine insights that stirred their communities while honoring liturgical practices and traditions. These figures embraced divine revelations that, although unique in their manifestations, mirrored the broader Church's mystical and ascetic traditions. Such examples lend credence to the universal nature of divine revelations, reinforcing that the integration of Luisa Piccarreta's teachings within the broader Catholic tradition is not an anomaly but part of a historical continuum.

Moving to the Renaissance period, the prophetic revelations given to Saint Vincent Ferrer provide another remarkable parallel. Proclaimed a miracle worker and preacher of the Last Judgment, Vincent's divine missions were thoroughly investigated and ultimately affirmed by Church authorities. His teachings, steeped in urgent calls for repentance and reform, invigorated a spiritually languid era, much like how the Divine Will messages aspire to rejuvenate contemporary faith and practice.

Even in more recent history, the Divine Mercy revelations to Saint Faustina Kowalska echo the enduring theme of merciful divine interventions seeking to refresh and sustain the Sacred Tradition. Despite initial ecclesiastical hesitations, the Church's eventual promulgation of Divine Mercy Sunday underlines a consistent pattern: authentic divine revelations, when properly discerned and aligned with Church teachings, invariably enrich the spiritual landscape. Faustina's diary, much pondered and validated, offers an enduring legacy that mirrors the hopeful trajectory anticipated for the Book of Heaven.

The analytical rigor applied to these historical cases underscores the cautious yet open stance the Church maintains regarding new private revelations. This pattern offers assurance to the faithful regarding Luisa Piccarreta's writings. Her documented experiences, when juxtaposed with those of past mystics who have similarly expanded the Church's understanding of divine realities, highlight an ongoing dialogue between Heaven and Earth. This dialogue, hallowed by tradition yet ever-whispering new depths, is both a testament to and a call for a more profound spiritual synergy.

Moreover, the cases of Saint Catherine of Siena and Saint Hildegard of Bingen, both received as prophets in their eras, signify how the Church embraces divine revelations that reveal profound theological insights. Catherine's dialogues with God, directing her to plead for Church reform, and Hildegard's intricate visions uniting the cosmos with divine harmony, found their places within the heart of Christendom. These cases illustrate that revelations like those experienced by Luisa Piccarreta are not only possible but can profoundly influence and coalesce with Sacred Tradition.

In conclusion, the historical cases of divine revelations examined here illuminate the Church's time-honored pattern of discerning, embracing, and ultimately integrating Heavenly mandates within the sacred tradition. These precedents offer assurance and a guiding framework for comprehending the revelations imparted to Luisa Piccarreta. The merging of Divine Will with Sacred Tradition is not a divergence but a continuation, a sublime extension of God's eternal plan manifesting within the historical and spiritual journey of the Church. As we contemplate these historical cases, we draw strength and wisdom, realizing that Luisa's messages stand on the solid ground of precedent and promise.

Chapter 15: Growing In Virtue Through The Divine Will

In the sacred journey towards holiness, to grow in virtue through the Divine Will is to immerse ourselves entirely in the profound abyss of God's love and providence. As we surrender our human will and align our hearts with the Divine Will, virtues blossom within us, like celestial flowers nurtured by the rays of divine grace. This transformative process ensconces the soul in virtuous habits, elevating even the most mundane aspects of life into holy acts. Through daily acts of obedience, humility, and love, fortified by the teachings revealed to Luisa Piccarreta in the Book of Heaven, the believer's soul begins to mirror the divine virtues of our Lord. This sacred union, borne of trust and surrender, fosters an intimate relationship with the Creator, making every moment a testament to divine glory. Thus, the journey to virtue is not merely a path to personal sanctification but also an echo of Heaven on earth, resounding through the lives of those who wholly embrace the Divine Will.

Practical Applications

In the hallowed pursuit of virtue, the teachings found within the Book of Heaven extend beyond mere theological musings, presenting themselves as guideposts for our daily lives. To live in the Divine Will is to weave an intricate tapestry of actions, thoughts, and emotions, all directed towards glorifying God and fostering personal sanctity. Thus, let us delve into the myriad ways in which this celestial doctrine can be fruitfully applied in the mundane corridors of our existence.

Foremost, the apostolate of daily sacrifice mustn't be disregarded. Each act, no matter how trivial, when imbued with the Divine Will, transforms into an offering of priceless worth. The preparation of a humble repast, the earnest completion of daily labor, or the patient endurance of life's vicissitudes—each becomes an opportunity to unite with the Divine, invoking sanctifying grace upon oneself and the world. Our Blessed Lord admonished that in the surrender of the will and the embrace of His Divine Will, the mundane transcends its ordinary confines, acquiring a celestial significance.

We must recall that the acquisition of virtue entails emulating the life of our Savior, Jesus Christ, and His Most Holy Mother, the Virgin Mary. Within their sufferings, joys, and everyday tasks, they constantly aligned their will with the Divine. Following we can cultivate virtues such as humility, patience, and charity by conscientiously aligning even the smallest facets of our lives with God's Will. This conscious surrender demands vigilance, devotion, and an ever-present awareness of His divine promptings.

The discipline of regular prayer holds paramount importance. Structured contemplative practices, such as the Divine Office or the Holy Rosary, immerse us within the rhythm of divine love. Through these prayers, the soul synchronizes with God's eternal cadence, drawing strength and wisdom requisite for the virtuous life. Additionally, spontaneous prayers of the heart throughout the day, seeking divine guidance in moments of ambiguity or peril, fortify one's resolve to live steadfastly within His Will.

Let not the search for convenience veer us from the path of righteousness. The application of the Divine Will in one's professional undertakings is an exquisite form of spiritual maturation. Executing one's vocational duties with integrity, excellence, and an unwavering commitment to moral principles cultivates virtues of diligence, honesty, and justice. Thus do we transform our workplaces into arenas of divine grace, where every interaction and duty completed reflects the sanctity of our Lord's earthly ministry.

Moreover, the engagement in corporal works of mercy, as mandated by the Gospel, serves as an essential application of divine will. Acts of charity, whether they manifest in feeding the hungry, sheltering the homeless, or comforting the sorrowful, demonstrate the tangible love of God. By offering our resources, time, and, more importantly, our presence, we incarnate Christ's love in our communities. Such endeavors, when executed with a heart aligned to the Divine Will, ascend to Heaven as precious sacrifices.

Equally essential is the stewardship of relationships, both within the familial enclave and beyond. Emulating Christ in our interactions with others fosters virtues of charity, patience, and forgiveness. In moments of strife or conflict, surrendering our pride and seeking reconciliation reflects the peace that surpasses all understanding, which is available when one lives in the Divine Will. It is within the crucible of relationships that virtues can be most rigorously tested and refined.

Educational apostolate, too, finds its place under the banner of the Divine Will. Educating the young and catechizing the ignorant are sacred duties. By imparting divine truths with zeal and clarity, we contribute to the sanctification not only of individuals but of society at large. To teach is to emulate the Divine Teacher, Christ Himself, who imparted truths eternal and immutable. Thus, in the arena of education, one finds numerous avenues to practice virtues such as patience, wisdom, and fortitude.

Venturing into the broader society, our engagement in civic responsibilities serves as another stage where virtue can truly shine. Participating in the political process, advocating for justice and the common good, and obeying lawful authority manifest virtues of justice, prudence, and temperance. Through active participation, we infuse the temporal order with divine principles, encapsulating the vision of a society that glorifies God in its statutes and practices.

In the context of suffering, which no mortal can evade, adherence to the Divine Will offers not just solace but transformative power. Enduring tribulations with grace and offering them up in union with Christ's Passion purifies the soul and fosters deep internal virtues such as humility, patience, and fortitude. Suffering accepted and borne with divine resignation can become a potent vehicle for divine grace, sanctifying not only the sufferer but also those who witness their fidelity.

The sacramental life, heart of the Catholic experience, must also be saturated with the Divine Will. Regular confession and frequent reception of the Holy Eucharist nourish the soul, cleansing it of sin and fortifying it for the journey towards perfection. Here, the virtues of repentance, gratitude, and love find their most compelling expressions. Through these sacraments, we receive divine grace, strengthening our resolve to live in alignment with God's Will.

Furthermore, the practice of fasting and penance cannot be overlooked. These disciplines of self-denial, when undertaken within the scope of the Divine Will, serve as powerful tools for spiritual refinement. They cultivate virtues of temperance, self-control, and humility, detaching us from worldly attachments and orienting our desires toward the divine. Thus, we emulate Christ's own forty-day fast in the desert, preparing our souls to resist temptation and achieve sanctity.

Finally, it is imperative to approach the Book of Heaven with an open heart and mind, allowing its pages to imbue our spirits with divine insight. Regular study and meditation upon its revelations guide the soul towards a deeper understanding and more profound application of the Divine Will. As one ponders its celestial wisdom, the virtues of wisdom, discernment, and faith blossom, equipping the faithful to live ever more fully in concordance with God's eternal plan.

Thus, the celestial roadmap provided through the Divine Will is not a distant abstraction but a living, breathing testament that invites us to transform every aspect of our lives. From the mundane tasks of daily existence to the profound sufferings that shape our spiritual journey, we are called to infuse everything with the light of the Divine Will, growing in virtue, and drawing ever closer to the heart of God.

Testimonials Of Change

Within these sacred texts and heavenly revelations, we find our hearts being gently guided towards a life more devout and virtuous. In examining the lives of those touched by the Divine Will, we bear witness to profound transformations, akin to the soul's journey from darkness into unquenchable light. How deeply moving are the testimonials that herald such divinely orchestrated metamorphoses! They offer indubitable proof of the Book of Heaven's power and the real presence of God at work.

"Ah, my life was a barren desert," says Clare, her eyes alight with newfound purpose. "When I discovered the writings of Luisa Piccarreta and began living in the Divine Will, it was as if the arid wasteland of my soul bloomed into a verdant garden." Clare's testimony reflects a recurring motif: lives once void of true spiritual nourishment becoming blossoming havens through the embrace of God's Divine Will.

If we ponder the shifting of the human heart in these narratives, the change is often described as miraculous and immediate, yet intricate. Matthew, a devout husband and father, recounts how his journey with the Divine Will offered profound insights into the unity desired by Christ, especially within the sacrosanct institution of marriage. "Our marriage, once fraught with discord, has been transformed. Now, the Divine Will is the anchor that holds us together. Where once there was strife, now blooms a peace that can only come from above," he shares, his voice imbued with solemn joy and gratitude.

Observe also the inherent humility that accompanies such divine conversion. Marie, a simple parishioner, who once felt insignificant in the grand tapestry of God's creation, found her sacred purpose through studying the Book of Heaven. "My sense of worth was not of this earth, but heavenly," she confides. "In embracing the Divine Will, I discovered that each small act of mine, when united with Jesus, takes on divine value." Her newfound purpose underscores the infinite worth placed upon every servant of the Lord, as seen through God's eyes.

Consider John's story, reminiscent of classic tales of prodigal sons. His life's path was one paved with rebellion and doubt, until he came upon Luisa Piccarreta's volumes. "The words were like a balm to my soul, directing me back to the Father's heart," he recounts. "I had strayed far, but the Divine Will brought me back to the fold, offering a grace I thought lost to me forever." The power of spiritual literature to act as both beacon and balm cannot be overstated, and it is through these accounts that we truly grasp the reach of God's love.

Such personal testimonies do not merely recount individual sanctifications but serve as living hagiographies that exalt the Divine Will's efficacy. Indeed, families, communities, and parishes have experienced collective rejuvenation under its influence. An entire parish in Southern Italy has been revitalized, as shared by their local priest, Father Antonio. "Our parish was spiritually dormant," he recalls, "but the introduction of Luisa's teachings on the Divine Will sparked a collective rekindling of faith. It is as if the Holy Spirit breathed new life into dry bones."

Among the most touching testimonials are those that involve the youth, for in their hearts, the future of our faith is tenderly cradled. Young Teresa, a high school student, openly shares her renewed commitment to purity and chastity after engaging with the Divine Will. "In a world that clamors for our attention and often leads us astray, these teachings have become my compass," she explains with youthful earnestness. "They guide me, not just in grand decisions, but in quotidian choices, shaping me into the person God intends me to be."

Moreover, the elderly find not a conclusion but a new beginning through such divine transformation. Teresa's grandmother, who once struggled with despair in her twilight years, shares her testament of renewed hope. "I thought my time of usefulness was over, but the Divine Will has imbued my life with purpose and peace." Both grandmother and grandchild testify to the cross-generational impact of living in the Divine Will, revealing the timeless nature of divine transformation.

It is not merely emotional or spiritual healing that many testify to; physical healings have also been recounted. Sarah, a mother of three, was diagnosed with a debilitating illness. The strength she derived from the Divine Will gave her an unshakable resilience. "I immersed myself in the teachings and began to feel a peace that surpassed understanding. My physical ailments, while still present, became bearable only through the miraculous strength granted by aligning with His Will."

Let us not forget those who tread paths of professional vocation that require them to embody the Divine Will in challenging environments. Paul, a surgeon, shares how he invokes the Divine Will before every procedure. "Every time I step into an operating room, I pray for my hands to be instruments of His Divine Will. The outcomes have been nothing short of miraculous," he reveals, conveying the importance of divine invocation even in our earthly professions.

Indeed, these testimonials of change offer not just inspiration but validation. They solidify the truth of the Book of Heaven, proving its divinely revealed nature and the transformative impact it imparts upon those willing to surrender wholly to God's Will. As we draw these personal stories into the grand narrative unfurling within the axiom, 'Thy will be done on earth as it is in heaven,' we find a community resurrected, individuals deeply sanctified, and souls eternally grateful.

Thus, the testimonials of change reveal the fruitfulness of walking in the light of the Divine Will, embodying virtues that set hearts ablaze with holy fervor, mirroring the celestial light from which they stem. The sacred revelations to Luisa Piccarreta do more than enlighten; they sanctify, creating a ripple that touches one life and flows effortlessly into another, binding them all in the endless harmony of God's Divine Symphony.

Chapter 16: Faith Strengthened By Divine Will

Amidst the tapestry of sacred tradition and celestial revelations, we discover that faith, when intertwined with the Divine Will, becomes an unshakable bastion of spiritual fortitude. In this harmonious union, the soul finds a celestial anchor, unwavering even in the fiercest tempests of doubt. The Divine Will, as revealed to Luisa Piccarreta, illuminates the path with divine clarity, dispelling the shadows that obscure the heart's understanding. In embracing the Divine Will, the believer is not merely adhering to divine precepts but is enveloped in a profound grace that invigorates and sustains. With each act of surrender, one's faith is not only reaffirmed but elevated to heights hitherto unknown, a testament to the transformative power of God's eternal plan. This divine orchestration assures the faithful that within God's grand design, every trial and tribulation serves to beckon the soul closer to the divine embrace, reinforcing the pillars of faith with the indomitable will of the Creator.

Building Strong Foundations

In the grand endeavor to build a life rooted firmly in the Divine Will, the importance of laying strong and unwavering foundations cannot be overstated. This process is akin to the meticulous construction of a cathedral, where every stone, every arch, and every stained glass window speaks to the glory and majesty of the sacred edifice. So too must our spiritual edifice be constructed with great care, guided by the teachings and revelations contained within the Book of Heaven.

The cornerstone of these foundations lies in the understanding and acceptance of the Divine Will as revealed through Luisa Piccarreta. Embracing this celestial wisdom requires not only intellectual assent but a wholehearted commitment to live in accordance with God's Eternal Fiat. This divine alignment infuses our daily lives with purpose and holiness, transforming the mundane into acts of divine significance.

At the heart of building these firm foundations is the adoption of a life of prayer and contemplation. Consider the mystic revelations given to Luisa, where she was invited into continuous dialogue with our Lord. Through her writings, we are invited to participate in this divine intimacy. Let our prayers become not mere words, but heartfelt conversations with the Divine, deeply rooted in the spirit of humility and trust. This unceasing communion with God fortifies our spiritual structure, making it resilient against the storms of doubt and adversity.

Moreover, the practice of profound humility and obedience forms the bedrock upon which our spiritual edifice stands. Recall the words of Christ to Luisa: "Without humility, one cannot comprehend the Divine Will." Obedience to the divine precepts and teachings of the Church ensures that our spiritual journey remains aligned with God's plan. It is through this humility, acknowledging our own limitations and the infinite wisdom of God, that we prepare ourselves to receive the gifts of Divine Will.

A vital element in building these strong foundations is the diligent study and reflection on the Book of Heaven. This sacred text must not be approached as mere literature; instead, it should be viewed as a living document, a divine manuscript that guides and enlightens. Reflecting upon its teachings and allowing them to permeate our hearts and minds fortifies our spiritual foundation. This sacred wisdom becomes the mortar that binds each stone of our faith, ensuring durability and strength.

Integrating the revelations from the Book of Heaven with the Church's sacred traditions further solidifies our foundations. The Church, in her wisdom, has provided a rich tapestry of doctrine, tradition, and sacred rites that complement and enhance the teachings received by Luisa Piccarreta. They are not separate streams of grace but converging rivers that nourish the soul, leading it to deeper union with the Divine Will.

Additionally, the sacraments serve as divine reinforcements in our spiritual construction. Participation in the Eucharist, Confession, and other sacraments draws us into the very heart of God's grace, empowering us to live out the Divine Will with vigor and clarity. Every Eucharistic celebration is a renewal of our commitment to this holy way of life, a moment where heaven touches earth, infusing our souls with divine strength.

Equally important in this divine architecture is the cultivation of virtues such as faith, hope, and charity. These virtues, when nurtured through acts of will and love, become immovable pillars that support our entire being. Faith anchors us in trust and belief, hope propels us forward amid trials, and charity allows the love of God to emanate from us to others, reflecting the Divine Will's radiant light.

Furthermore, communal life within the Church enriches individual efforts. Engaging with fellow believers who are committed to living in the Divine Will offers support, encouragement, and shared wisdom. As iron sharpens iron, so does this holy fellowship refine and strengthen our spiritual edifice. Through communal worship, study groups, and acts of service, the faith of the community becomes an integral part of our individual foundations.

An unwavering devotion to the Blessed Virgin Mary also fortifies our spiritual journey. As the first and most perfect disciple of the Divine Will, Mary exemplifies perfect obedience and submission to God's plan. By entrusting ourselves to her maternal care and emulating her virtues, we anchor our foundations in the surest of soils, thus ensuring growth and stability in our spiritual lives.

Let not the heart be troubled by the trials and tribulations that seek to shake these divine foundations. Just as a well-constructed cathedral withstands the test of time and elements, so too will a soul fortified by the Divine Will remain steadfast through the vicissitudes of life. Such fortitude is borne not out of human strength but by the omnipotent grace of Almighty God, ever-present and ever-faithful.

In this sacred enterprise of strengthening our faith through the Divine Will, let us be diligent artisans. Let our efforts be marked by perseverance, our hearts by humility, and our minds by unwavering focus. With Christ as our divine architect and Luisa Piccarreta's revelations as our blueprint, we can construct a spiritual edifice that glorifies God, bears witness to His truth, and withstands the trials of this earthly pilgrimage.

Let every stone laid be a testament to our love and dedication to the Almighty. May our foundations, firmly rooted in prayer, sacrament, study, virtue, and communal fellowship, rise as a sanctified abode, prepared for the eternal indwelling of the Divine Will. Thus shall our journey, steeped in divine grace, lead us ever closer to the fulfillment of God's heavenly plan.

Overcoming Doubt

In the sacred crucible of faith, doubt often finds unwelcome ingress, testing the very foundations of our beliefs. Yet, through the compelling revelations of the Divine Will as espoused in the Book of Heaven, we find the means to transcend uncertainty. When grappling with doubt, one must invoke the pure flame of Divine Will, which illuminates the soul and dispels the shadows that cloud our spiritual vision.

One of the most profound insights from Luisa Piccarreta's revelations is the understanding that doubt is not an enemy, but rather a facet of the human condition that can ultimately fortify our faith. By facing the specter of doubt with courage, we deepen our reliance on God's divine providence. It is in these moments of uncertainty that we can most clearly perceive the guiding hand of the Divine Will, steering us back to the shores of unwavering belief.

In our journey with the Divine Will, understanding the nature of doubt is paramount. Doubt arises when human intellect grapples with the mysteries of faith and the ineffable nature of God's plans. The intricate revelations given to Luisa illuminate this struggle, showing us that the intellect alone cannot fathom the depths of divine mysteries.

Consider, for instance, the tale of the apostle Thomas, whose doubts were met not with rebuke but with an invitation to deeper understanding. The Lord's response to Thomas was not a condemnation but a compassionate extension of truth, "Reach hither thy finger, and behold my hands." (John 20:27) This divine patience with Thomas's incredulity serves as a template for us. It teaches that persistent doubt, when met with Divine Will, transforms into a fertile ground where faith can grow more robustly.

Moreover, the Book of Heaven asserts that the divine plan often eludes human comprehension not to confound us, but to call us to a higher trust. In our moments of doubt, we are prodded to transcend our limited understanding and lean more heavily upon God. This manner of trust is reflected in Luisa's writings, where she consistently emphasizes surrender to God's will as a path to spiritual enlightenment and serenity.

It is also essential to remember the manifold examples of saints who faced and overcame doubt through the power of faith. Saint Augustine, whose journey from skepticism to enduring faith serves as a testament, famously remarked, "Understanding is the reward of faith. Therefore, seek not to understand that thou mayest believe, but believe that thou mayest understand." In their lives, saints embodied the principle that overcoming doubt is a divine grace, cultivated by unwavering trust in God's omnipotence.

In our endeavor to overcome doubt, prayer becomes an indispensable ally. Engaging in heartfelt dialogue with the Divine not only fortifies our spirit but also invites celestial light to pierce through the clouded veil of skepticism. Through prayer, believers enter a divine communion, receiving the assurance that God's will is perpetually aligned with our highest good.

By embedding oneself in the teachings expounded in the Book of Heaven, one is gifted with perspectives that enable the transcendence of doubt. This sacred text acts as a conduit through which the Divine Will flows, alleviating the anxieties that often accompany human frailty. The revelations bestowed upon Luisa Piccarreta offer a lifeline, inviting the faithful to immerse themselves fully in the ocean of divine wisdom.

The Divine Will does not merely exist in abstract theology but is demonstrated through acts of divine intervention and the lived experiences of the faithful. Consider the testimonies of those whose lives have been markedly transformed by embracing the Divine Will. These personal accounts serve as empirical validations of the truths revealed within the Book of Heaven.

Equally, the sacraments stand as pillars of faith, anchoring believers in the assurance of God's mercy and love. Participation in the Eucharist, in particular, is an act of devotion that reaffirms one's alignment with Divine Will. This sacred rite, wherein the Bread of Life nourishes the soul, fortifies the believer against the insidious tendrils of doubt.

Moreover, the communal aspect of worship within the Church fosters a collective strength that can subsume individual doubts. The shared liturgical practices and mutual encouragement of fellow believers create an environment where faith is continually reinforced. It is within the sanctified walls of the Church that doubts are often laid to rest, as the collective faith of the community becomes a bulwark against individual uncertainties.

It cannot be overstated that the Divine Will invites us to a deeper participation in God's eternal plan. This invitation extends beyond mere intellectual assent to a dynamic engagement with divine grace. By continuously seeking to align our will with that of the Divine, we partake in the unfolding of God's kingdom on earth. The Book of Heaven guides the faithful through this process, providing the spiritual tools necessary to navigate the uncertainties of mortal life.

Furthermore, overcoming doubt involves a rejection of worldly distractions and an embrace of spiritual disciplines. The secular world, with its myriad philosophies and temporal concerns, often sows seeds of uncertainty. By cultivating habits of meditation, scriptural study, and regular sacramental participation, believers strengthen their defenses against such influences.

The experience of doubt is a crucible where faith is tested, refined, and ultimately affirmed. Through the teachings encapsulated in the Book of Heaven, believers are equipped to meet these challenges with confidence and grace. Embracing the Divine Will nurtures a resilience that transcends the ephemeral concerns of this world, anchoring the soul in the eternal truths of God's love and providence.

Indeed, the journey of overcoming doubt is not linear but rather a continual process of growth and renewal. As believers delve deeper into the Book of Heaven, they discover layers of divine wisdom that empower them to face new challenges with a fortified spirit. Each revelation serves as a beacon that lights the path of faith, guiding them ever closer to a full and joyous communion with God.

In summation, to overcome doubt is to embrace the Divine Will with unwavering trust, seeking enlightenment through prayer, scripture, and the sacraments. The Book of Heaven stands as a monumental testament to God's enduring love and guidance, offering the faithful a roadmap to spiritual certainty. With each step taken in faith, doubt is gradually vanquished, replaced by a profound and abiding trust in the Divine Will.

Chapter 17: Hope Fortified By The Book Of Heaven

As one delves steadfastly into the luminous "Book of Heaven," hope is girded anew, fortified by the celestial utterances bestowed upon Luisa Piccarreta. These divine revelations, laden with grace and truth, illuminate the path through life's adversities, affirming that hope, anchored in the Divine Will, transforms the soul to surmount even the direst of trials. Through the sagas of perseverance chronicled within its sacred pages, believers find not merely stories but divine encouragement, a covenant that whispers assurance of God's providence. In the beauty of these hallowed words, believers are beckoned to embrace a life enriched by divine promise, where each struggle is but a prelude to heavenly triumph, and the ultimate victory is the fulfillment of God's eternal plan.

Stories Of Perseverance

Amidst the burgeoning pages of the sacred text, The Book of Heaven, one finds not merely abstract doctrines but vivid, pulsating narratives that enshrine the quintessence of human resilience. These are the stories of individuals who have traversed the arid deserts of suffering, their spirits fortified by divine grace, reflecting the omnipotent hand of God guiding them through their darkest hours. Drawing from the luminous volumes penned by the prodigious Luisa Piccarreta, these tales stand as monumental edifices of faith and perseverance, testifying to the transforming power of living in the Divine Will.

Consider the chronicle of Anna, a devout woman whose life was marred by relentless afflictions. Bedridden by a debilitating illness that stripped her of physical autonomy, Anna sought solace in prayer and the writings of Luisa Piccarreta. The volumes became her daily bread, nourishing a soul ravaged by incessant pain. She found in them not just an echo of her suffering, but a divine invitation to unite her tribulations with the agonies of Christ. Anna's unwavering hope, stoked by The Book of Heaven, rekindled the flame of perseverance within her. Through the incessant whisperings of despair, she could discern the gentle murmur of God's promise—His Will done on earth as it is in Heaven.

Then there's the tale of Marcus, a man ensnared by the dark tendrils of addiction. For years, he wandered through life, seeking ephemeral pleasures that left his soul yearning and parched. Upon discovering the Divine Will Movement, and immersing himself in the sanctified text, Marcus found a beacon of light that pierced through his immense darkness. Each reading fortified his resolve, and the sacred narratives imbued him with the strength to wage war against his vices. His encounter with the profound revelations in The Book of Heaven transformed his spirit, anchoring him in a newfound purpose. His story is a testament to the redemptive power that lies in surrendering to the Divine Will.

Maria's journey is another testament to divine perseverance. Living in an era when socioeconomic barriers dictated the limits of one's existence, Maria's family faced destitution. With a heart weighed by the burdens of poverty, she could have easily succumbed to despair. However, her discovery of The Book of Heaven ignited within her an unyielding hope. The divine revelations became her refuge, instilling resilience and a steadfast trust in God's providence. Maria's prayer life deepened, intertwining her earthly sufferings with the celestial promises articulated in Luisa's writings. Her family's fortunes did not change overnight, but her spirit was lifted, transcending the shackles of her material hardships. This, in turn, impacted her family, nurturing an environment of unwavering faith and hope, even in the direst of circumstances.

Young Timothy, a lad impaired by an ailment that impeded his speech, found an unlikely mentor in the hallowed pages of The Book of Heaven. Mocked and ostracized by peers, Timothy's heart harbored a well of sorrow. His mute lips, however, were no barrier to the symphony of divine love he experienced upon delving into the writings of Luisa Piccarreta. The sacred texts spoke directly to his soul, unfettered by the confines of verbal communication. Timothy learned to offer his silent suffering as a fragrant oblation to the Divine Will, finding comfort in the realization that his pain was not in vain but a profound participation in Christ's own sufferings. His silent testimony became a powerful echo of God's unending grace, a beacon of hope for all who witnessed his unwavering peace.

The saga of Teresa, a mother burdened by the loss of a child, is another poignant story of perseverance. The weight of grief threatened to crush her spirit, yet she found refuge in the Divine Will. The verses in The Book of Heaven became her lifeline, tethering her to divine promises when earthly consolations faltered. Each sorrowful page she turned was imbued with a divine message of hope, a reminder that her child's soul rested in the eternal embrace of God. Teresa transformed her mourning into a sacred act of offering, drawing strength from the celestial words that transcended her temporal pain. Her journey from despair to divine serenity stands as a testament to the comforting embrace of the Divine Will, even amidst life's most harrowing losses.

John, a soldier scarred by the visceral horrors of war, returned home with a fractured spirit. Haunted by the specters of conflict, he struggled to reintegrate into his once-normal life. It was through The Book of Heaven that John found a pathway to healing. The powerful messages of love, sacrifice, and divine purpose enshrined within the text resonated deeply with his wounded soul. The sacred writings guided him to not only forgive himself but also to see his suffering as part of a larger, divine blueprint intricately woven by God. John's tale is an indomitable example of how the Divine Will can heal even the deepest scars left by human strife.

Amidst these narratives, the common thread is a profound surrender to the Divine Will as illuminated in The Book of Heaven. This surrender does not imply a passive acceptance of suffering but an active engagement with the divine, transforming temporal sorrows into eternal victories. Each story echoes the perennial truth that perseverance, anchored in divine revelation, is not merely an act of enduring but a transcendent journey towards sanctification.

These accounts also shine a light on the indomitable spirit of Luisa Piccarreta herself. This humble servant, chosen by divine grace to channel messages of celestial import, exemplifies the very notion of perseverance. Her life, marked by physical afflictions and spiritual trials, stands as a monumental testament to the sanctifying power of living in the Divine Will. Through her writings, legions of souls have found their struggles mirrored and their hopes rekindled.

Thus, Stories of Perseverance in the realm of the Book of Heaven are more than mere historical anecdotes; they are living parables that continue to inspire and fortify believers. They showcase not only the transforming power of the Divine Will but also how it serves as a divine anchor amidst the tempests of life. As we reflect upon these sacred journeys, we are reminded that the path of divine surrender, though fraught with trials, ultimately leads to an eternal communion with the Divine.

In this tapestry of faith and endurance, The Book of Heaven is the golden thread that weaves through the lives of those who dare to embrace the Divine Will. It transforms their earthly trials into heavenly triumphs, their mundane sufferings into sacred offerings. And therein lies the profound beauty of these stories of perseverance—each one a luminous testament to God's unwavering promise and infinite love.

Encouragement For Believers

In the luminous pages of the "Book of Heaven," there lies an abundance of divine words that beckon believers toward a fortified hope. This sacred volume, dictated by our Lord to the humble and pious soul of Luisa Piccarreta, offers a path of spiritual elevation and a wellspring of encouragement. Dive with me into this ocean of celestial truths, where hope is not merely sustained but gloriously magnified.

Those who tread upon the sacred journey of the Divine Will often encounter the tempests of doubt and despondency. Yet, it is precisely within these trials that the promises of Our Lord, revealed to Luisa, become beacons of unwavering light. The Book of Heaven, as dictated by the Divine Master, assures us that every sorrow, every cross, endowed with His Will, transforms into a treasure of inestimable grace.

Consider the words of comfort from our Savior, where He elucidates that each act performed in His Divine Will possesses an eternal echo, resonating within Heaven's chambers and yielding fruit that shall never perish. With such assurances, dear believers, how can one falter? How can one's heart not swell with hope, knowing that even the smallest act of love and obedience is cherished and magnified by the Almighty?

Moreover, the communion of saints, a profound and often invigorating aspect of our faith, aligns itself splendidly with the teachings of the Divine Will. We see in the lives of saints like Saint Therese and our own Blessed Mother, a perfect conformity to the Divine Will, which led them to joy amidst suffering and triumph over worldly concerns. As you contemplate these holy examples, let your spirit be stirred with enthusiasm, for the same path is laid out before you, rich with divine promises and heavenly rewards.

Imagine the tender dialogues between Luisa and Jesus, where Christ Himself reassures her and, through her, all of humanity, that His Will is the safest refuge, the most secure fortress against the vicissitudes of life. "Do not fear," He says, "For My Will is a shelter from all that can harm." Such words are not ephemeral consolations but everlasting truths, meant to embolden every soul who seeks the heights of divine union.

Indeed, the cultivation of hope is a symphony composed of faith, trust, and divine assurances. Every page of the "Book of Heaven" echoes with the harmonious interplay of God's promises and the believer's journey. As you read and meditate upon these heavenly revelations, you are invited to partake in this celestial melody, to resonate with the symphony that transforms despair into jubilant hope.

Let us remember, too, the significance of communal prayer and intercessory support among believers. The Divine Will Movement is not a solitary endeavor but a collective pilgrimage. As such, the encouragement received from fellow pilgrims, sharing in the same divine aspirations, is indispensable. As Saint Paul reminds us in his letters, "Encourage one another and build each other up." A community vested in the Divine Will becomes a bastion of mutual support, uplifting each heart with the shared goal of divine fulfilment.

The sacraments, those sacred channels of divine grace, also play a pivotal role in fostering hope among believers. Participation in the Eucharist, Confession, and the Anointing of the Sick provides not only spiritual nourishment but a reaffirmation of God's promises revealed in the "Book of Heaven." These sacraments are celestial bridges, guiding the faithful back to the Divine Will and enveloping them in God's comforting embrace. In times of turmoil, such as illness or moral trials, let the sacraments rejuvenate your spirit and strengthen your resolve.

Let the words within this sacred text kindle within you a blazing fire of perseverance. Christ's revelations to Luisa continually emphasize that the path of Divine Will, albeit strewn with trials, inevitably leads to a horizon of radiant glory. Each step, every act of trust and surrender, brings you closer to the ultimate union with His Will. Rejoice, for you do not walk alone; Christ Himself guides you, His hand ever extended to lift you from the shadows.

In reflecting upon the lives transformed by these divine revelations, consider testimonials of change heralded by the "Book of Heaven." From ordinary believers who found extraordinary courage, to souls in desolation who discovered boundless hope, these narratives are testaments to the profound impact of divine truth on the human soul. Each story is a beacon, a testimony to the transformative power of living in the Divine Will.

Luisa's own life stands as a towering testament to the efficacy of God's promises. Despite her physical sufferings and humble exterior, she possessed an unwavering hope kindled by her intimate union with the Divine Will. Her persistent faith, her steadfastness in suffering, and her eventual glorification, urge believers to embrace the Divine Will with similar fervor and trust. If a soul so hidden and simple could be so exalted, what, then, is not possible for each of you?

The challenges of modern life, filled with unforeseen trials and uncertainties, often assail our spiritual resolve. Yet the Divine Will, as elucidated in the Book of Heaven, offers a perennial source of strength and hope. Believers are reminded that each moment of surrender, sanctified by divine intention, shapes a future radiant with divine grace. With hope as your armor and the Divine Will as your compass, navigate life's labyrinth with renewed courage and serenity.

Dear hearts, as you ponder upon these sacred revelations, let your soul be enveloped by the boundless love of Christ. Let the encouragement found within these pages emblazon your spirit with hope unshakeable. The path of the Divine Will, illuminated by the "Book of Heaven," is a journey toward an eternal embrace of divine love and ultimate beatitude. In every trial, in every triumph, know that hope rests firmly in the promises of Our Lord, ever faithful, ever true.

- Trust in the Divine Will, for it is the true path to joy.
- Draw upon the sacraments as sources of divine strength.
- Seek the support of fellow believers in times of doubt.
- Allow the examples of saints and Luisa to inspire your journey.

Thus, fortified by these divine assurances, let your journey in the Divine Will be one of hope and triumph. The celestial truths espoused within the "Book of Heaven" are not mere words; they are living promises, breathed forth by God Himself to lead you toward eternal bliss. With each act in the Divine Will, each embrace of divine love, march boldly forward, for He who has promised is ever faithful. In His Divine Will, your hope shall be eternally fortified.

Chapter 18: Love Deepened Through Sacred Teachings

Love, in its most sublime form, is enkindled by the sacred teachings bestowed upon humanity through divine revelation, and nowhere is this more profoundly captured than within the pages of the Book of Heaven. Herein, Christ Himself illuminates the path of charity, urging the faithful to transcend earthly bonds and embrace the all-encompassing love that mirrors His own Sacred Heart. Each act of charity performed in alignment with the Divine Will becomes a conduit for heavenly grace, transforming mere mortals into vessels of God's infinite love. As we delve into these teachings, we find that love is not merely an emotion but a divine command, an eternal call to reflect the boundless compassion of our Savior. In the practice of these teachings, love ceases to be an ephemeral sentiment and is instead anchored in the eternal truths of our faith, urging us to love not as the world loves, but as Christ commands: with utmost purity, selflessness, and spiritual fervor.

Acts Of Charity

To comprehend the grandeur of the Divine Will, one must delve into its practical manifestations, which are replete with the rich acts of charity ordained by sacred teachings. Charity, in its truest form, encompasses more than mere almsgiving; it is the heart's resonance with God's infinite love, an echo of divine harmony that seeks to alleviate the suffering and uplift the spirits of others.

What can be more sublime than imitating Christ's boundless compassion? In His Divine Will, every action undertaken in charity becomes a luminous beacon, resplendent with grace. The Book of Heaven fervently illuminates this principle, illustrating that acts of charity are not merely good deeds but sacramental acts, imbued with divine intent, purifying both the giver and the receiver.

Luisa Piccarreta's revelations reveal that by living in the Divine Will, one's capacity for charity is immensely amplified. The heart attuned to God's Will becomes a conduit of divine mercy, its love flowing with inextinguishable fervor. In committing to charity, one partakes in God's redemptive mission, embodying Christ's tender mercy and eternal love.

Consider the tale of the poor widow, who, in spite of her meager means, shared her last loaf with a stranger. Her act of charity, small in worldly reckoning, became a profound testament of faith. It is precisely these acts, however modest, that herald God's kingdom on earth. The Book of Heaven asserts that charity performed in union with the Divine Will reaches celestial heights, dispersing blessings that transcend time and space.

Indeed, charity, forged in divine alignment, transcends mere social obligation. It becomes the soul's homage to the Creator, a perpetuation of the Incarnation where the eternal Word took flesh to serve and save humanity. This union of divine will and human action epitomizes the theological virtues of faith, hope, and love, underscoring that charity is not optional but essential for those yearning to live in the Divine Will.

Moreover, The Book of Heaven elucidates that acts of charity are sacrificial, necessitating a relinquishment of self for the elevation of another. In this divine economy, the granaries of heaven overflow, for every act of charity, no matter how inconspicuous, enriches the eternal treasury. The soul, engaging in such acts, finds itself ever more conformed to Christ, the Supreme Exemplar of charity.

Take, for instance, the countless anecdotes of saints who embodied these sacred teachings. Saint Therese of Lisieux, small in stature yet mighty in spirit, committed to the 'little way,' offering every moment, every suffering, every joy as an act of love. Her life, punctuated by numerous acts of charity, radiated the light of Christ. Such examples beckon us to emulate that divine simplicity and profound charity.

The Divine Will requires that charity be performed with a pure heart, devoid of selfish ambition. The giver must relinquish all attachments to accolades or worldly recognition. Genuine charity, as Sacred Tradition proclaims, emanates from an unadulterated love for God and neighbor. The Book of Heaven reiterates this by revealing that acts of charity, when performed in purity, become channels of divine grace, furthering God's redemptive work on earth.

In this light, charity becomes both a mystical and practical reality. As the hands extend to give, the heart ascends in worship, and the soul partakes in the eternal liturgy of love. The profound simplicity of such acts belies their immense spiritual significance. Each charitable deed, though cloaked in humility, resounds in heaven's halls, where angels and saints exult in the ever-present echo of God's love.

Luisa's writings vividly convey that charity in the Divine Will is transformative. It heals wounds, secures peace, and fosters a communion of souls. As believers strive to actualize these teachings, every act of charity becomes a conduit for divine encounter. It is through such acts that the Divine Will manifests concretely, weaving a tapestry of grace interspersed with threads of human and divine cooperation.

The beauty of charity lies in its duality; it serves both the physical and spiritual needs of its beneficiaries. As saints and scholars have attested, to feed the hungry, clothe the naked, and visit the imprisoned are corporeal mercies, reflecting the corporeal acts of Christ. Yet, to counsel the doubtful, comfort the sorrowful, and pray for the living and the dead are spiritual mercies, showcasing the very heart of God.

In pursuit of deepening love through sacred teachings, every act of charity becomes a milestone on the path to divine friendship. The Divine Will enjoins us to see Christ in every person, to serve as if serving Him directly. This profound realization engenders a love that is sacrificial, unconditional, and unceasing. Reflect upon how St. John of the Cross articulated it - "In the evening of life, we will be judged on love alone."

Those who embrace the Divine Will find themselves enveloped in a divine mandate to love indefatigably. Picture a church community, motivated by the Book of Heaven, engaging in acts of charity. Shelters are built, the hungry are fed, the lonely find companionship. Their unified effort becomes a living testament to the transformative power of divine love, reinforcing that heaven's work is indeed done on earth when hearts align with God's Will.

In closing, the sacred teachings emphasize that acts of charity, inspired by the Divine Will, transcend mere philanthropy. They become sacred offerings, fountains of grace that sanctify both giver and receiver. True charity is the very breath of the Divine Will, filling the world with tangible expressions of God's love. By adhering to these sacred commands, believers not only fulfill divine mandates but partake in an eternal symphony of love, echoing from Heaven to earth and back again.

Loving As Christ Commands

In the brilliance of Christ's divine light, our understanding of love expands beyond human comprehension. To love as Christ commands is not merely to engage in acts of charity or to hold affectionate feelings for one another. It is a profound, sacred duty, entrenched in the very essence of the Divine Will as revealed to us through the celestial teachings of Luisa Piccarreta. For as we delve into the Book of Heaven, our hearts are indelibly marked by Christ's own example, which beckons us to a love that transcends earthly bounds.

Our Lord's commands concerning love are both simple and demanding: "Love one another as I have loved you." This decree, though direct in its wording, carries with it the ineffable weight of Christ's own sacrificial love. His love was exemplified by His passion, death, and resurrection, a trinity of moments that forever changed the course of human history and set a divine standard for all aspiring followers. To emulate such love, one must engage not only in outward actions but inward transformation, allowing the heart to be molded by the sacred teachings of the Divine Will.

To love as Christ commands is to encapsulate the virtues of patience, humility, and infinite mercy. It is to imbue our daily interactions with the same grace that Christ showed to all He encountered. In the Divine Will Movement, as instructed by Piccarreta, these virtues are not hypothetical ideals but lived realities. They shape the very nature of our existence, beckoning us to rise above our limitations and embrace a supernatural form of love.

This calls for a deep alignment with Christ's own heart, where His desires become our own. It is through the continual practice of the Divine Will that we are able to attune ourselves to this level of spiritual intimacy. As we surrender our will, moment by moment, to God's Divine Will, we begin to mirror the love of Christ more authentically in our lives. This surrender, however, is neither passive nor devoid of effort. It requires a vigorous engagement with our faith, a consistent aligning of our choices with the divine precepts bestowed upon us.

The journey of loving as Christ commands is akin to a pilgrimage, one that is both arduous and rewarding. As we traverse the path illuminated by the sacred texts revealed to Piccarreta, we are continually reminded of Christ's ultimate sacrifice. Each step invites us to die to ourselves, to our ego and our desires, so that Christ's love might reign supreme in our hearts. This is not an instantaneous transformation but a gradual transfiguration, wherein every act of kindness, every deed of humility, becomes a testament to our deepened capacity for divine love.

Moreover, this journey is marked by an unwavering commitment to the community. Christ's command for love is inherently communal. It binds us to one another in a tapestry of divine interdependence. As Roman Catholics, our participation in the sacraments, particularly the Eucharist, nurtures this communal bond, reminding us of our unity in the body of Christ. Each act of charity, each gesture of love, thus becomes a thread that strengthens the fabric of our ecclesial community.

Reflecting on the teachings of the Book of Heaven, we find that Christ's love is not a mere sentiment but an active force—a divine imperative that compels us to transform every aspect of our lives. In the writings of Piccarreta, we are exhorted to embrace this love with a wholehearted fervor. It calls us to go beyond mere compliance with the commandments, to embody the spirit of divine love in its fullness. This embodiment is made manifest in our actions, in the sacrifices we make for others, and in the serene acceptance of God's will in all circumstances.

In the endeavor to love as Christ commands, we also encounter the necessity of forgiveness. Christ's love is redemptive; it forgives and restores. The Divine Will Movement places significant emphasis on this aspect of love, urging us to forgive as we have been forgiven. This forgiveness is comprehensive, extending not only to others but to ourselves. It is through the grace of divine forgiveness that we are liberated from the shackles of resentment and are made free to love authentically and unconditionally.

Additionally, the sacred teachings reveal that loving as Christ commands involves a deep-seated joy, a joy that is not contingent upon external circumstances but rooted in the divine assurance of God's love for us. This joy is both a fruit and a mark of genuine love. It is present in the midst of trials and tribulations, serving as a beacon of hope and a witness to the transformative power of divine love. The Divine Will, as shared through the revelations to Luisa Piccarreta, invites us to cultivate this joy and to let it permeate every action, every thought, and every interaction we have.

Our devotion to loving as Christ commands ultimately leads us to a destiny of eternal union with God. The Book of Heaven, in its profound depths, offers us a glimpse of this divine union—a foretaste of heaven. As we emulate Christ's love, we participate in the divine life, experiencing a communion with God that transcends the limitations of our earthly existence. This communion is not reserved for the afterlife but is a present reality, accessible to all who earnestly seek to live in accordance with the Divine Will.

Thus, in our quest to love as Christ commands, we are perpetually guided by the luminous teachings inscribed in the Book of Heaven. These sacred revelations illuminate our path, revealing the beauty and majesty of a life lived in full accord with God's divine desires. Through fervent prayer, unwavering faith, and diligent practice of the Divine Will, we are drawn ever closer to fulfilling the sublime command to love as our Lord has loved us.

Chapter 19: Fruits Of The Divine Will Movement

The Divine Will Movement bears its fruits abundantly, as the lives transformed testify with fervent devotion. In the embrace of Divine Will, souls find a celestial harmony, aligning their daily lives with the divine desires of the Almighty. Personal stories abound where hearts, once burdened by worldly woes, soar with spiritual liberty, finding peace and purpose in surrendering to this divine dance. Communities, too, flourish, bound by the shared joy of living in God's Will, and fostering unity that radiates Christ's love. These testimonies are the glowing embers of a holy fire, igniting faith and kindling virtuous living within the hearts of the faithful, bringing forth a harvest of divine grace unparalleled in its magnificence. The fruits of this sacred movement reveal not just personal sanctification but weave an intricate tapestry of communal transformation, echoing the omnipotent symphony of God's eternal love and mercy.

Personal Stories

Within the hallowed embrace of the Divine Will movement, countless souls have found their lives transformed in ways both profound and humble. The testimonies of these individuals, who have journeyed alongside the spiritual guidance of Luisa Piccarreta's writings, shine as luminous beacons. These stories speak to the fruitfulness of living in the Divine Will, fulfilling the Lord's prayer that "Thy will be done on earth as it is in heaven."

Consider the life of Isabella, a devout Catholic whose days were once marked by a sense of spiritual longing. Isabella had diligently adhered to the sacraments and the teachings of the Church, yet she felt an unfulfilled yearning, a desire for a more intimate communion with the Divine. It was through a small study group dedicated to the Book of Heaven that Isabella was introduced to Luisa's writings. The revelations and teachings within those volumes resonated with an unmistakable clarity, sparking a transformation within her soul.

Isabella began to immerse herself in the Divine Will, endeavoring to align her actions, thoughts, and prayers with the will of God. Her spiritual life blossomed as she devoted herself to prayer, meditation, and acts of charity imbued with the intention of the Divine Will. This transformation did not go unnoticed by those around her; her friends and family observed a newfound peace, joy, and purpose emanating from her. Isabella's testimony is one among many that illustrate how the Divine Will movement has borne rich fruit in the lives of the faithful.

Another remarkable tale comes from a gentleman named Gregory, once a man beset by an overwhelming sense of purposelessness. Despite his outward success and the comforts of a prosperous life, Gregory felt an inner void that nothing in the temporal world could fill. He stumbled upon the Book of Heaven during a pilgrimage to a Marian shrine, and the teachings he discovered within its pages awakened within him a profound contemplation of divine mysteries.

Gregory's journey with the Divine Will marked a turning point in his life as he started participating in frequent Eucharist Adoration and became more deeply involved in parish activities. His encounters with the words of Jesus, as conveyed through Luisa Piccarreta, opened his heart to a life of service and humility. Gregory's transformation was not solely an inward journey; it manifested through his charitable works and dedication to spreading the Divine Will's message within his community. Through deeds both great and small, Gregory bore witness to the divine fruits of living in accordance with God's will.

Likewise, Sister Mary, a cloistered nun, recounts her journey into the Divine Will as the most significant spiritual awakening of her consecrated life. Despite her deep dedication to her vocation and her community, Sister Mary felt an intangible barrier to complete spiritual fulfillment. It was during a retreat focused on mystical theology that she was introduced to Luisa Piccarreta's revelations. As she delved deeper into the teachings, she recognized a calling to unite her will entirely with God's.

Sister Mary's experience with the Divine Will movement became a cornerstone of her spiritual and communal life. Her prayers and daily activities now carried an intentionality that sought to fuse heaven and earth, enriching her devotion and the quality of her intercessory prayers. The fruits of Sister Mary's transformation can be seen in her serene demeanor, the wisdom she imparts to younger nuns, and her unwavering commitment to living in the Divine Will.

The story of Marcus, a youthful seminarian, further illustrates the powerful influence of the Divine Will. Struggling with doubts and uncertainties about his vocation, Marcus was in a state of spiritual turmoil. It was providential that a fellow seminarian handed him a volume of Luisa's writings. As Marcus read and meditated upon the text, he found the answers to his queries and a renewed zest for his path.

Marcus's story is particularly noteworthy because it underscores the symbiotic relationship between youthful zeal and timeless divine wisdom. By embracing the Divine Will, Marcus gained not only theological insight but also the strength to persevere through trials, fortifying his resolve to serve God's Church. His persistence and joy became infectious among his peers, illustrating how the Divine Will can inspire and rejuvenate even those at the outset of their spiritual journey.

In addition, the account of Eleanor, a mother of five, bears testimony to the transformative power of the Divine Will in familial life. Eleanor, already a fervent believer, found herself yearning for a deeper spiritual life amidst the demands of motherhood. Through a parish book club, she discovered the writings of Luisa Piccarreta, which soon became central to her daily reflections and prayers.

Eleanor's family began participating in her newfound spiritual practices, including nightly prayers and engaging in acts of service enshrined by the Divine Will. Her home became a place of peace and spiritual growth, testifying to the sanctity that can be achieved in domestic life. The fruits of Eleanor's devotion are visible in the lives of her children, who embrace faith and virtue with marked enthusiasm and grace, highlighting the far-reaching impact of the Divine Will.

Then, we have the poignant experience of Brother Anthony, a monk grappling with a crisis of faith. For years, Brother Anthony had dedicated himself to monastic life, yet a veil of desolation clouded his spirit. In a moment of divine providence, Brother Anthony was given the Book of Heaven by another monk who had found solace within its pages. The profound and contemplative nature of the writings pierced his heart, guiding him toward a renewal of faith.

Through his immersion in the Divine Will, Brother Anthony experienced a rekindling of his spiritual fervor. His prayers became more profound, and his actions more aligned with divine intent. Brother Anthony's rediscovery of his vocation inspired his entire monastic community, fostering a collective commitment to live in Divine Will. The monastic life, once marked by routine, now thrived with a dynamic spiritual energy that nourished each member profoundly.

These personal stories, a mere glimpse into the myriad experiences of those touched by the Divine Will, collectively testify to the movement's divine fruitfulness. The transformative power of Luisa Piccarreta's revelations calls believers to deeper communion with God, urging them to surrender their wills to the Divine Will completely. Such surrender has manifested in lives characterized by peace, purpose, and profound spiritual fortitude, affirming the divine inspiration behind the Book of Heaven.

In recognizing and sharing these personal stories, the intricate tapestry of the Divine Will movement is revealed. Each thread, representing a life touched and transformed, contributes to a greater understanding of God's plan manifested through Luisa's writings. As believers continue to walk this divine path, the legacy of these transformations serves as both inspiration and testament to the miraculous and enduring power of the Divine Will.

Community Impact

The Divine Will Movement, heralded by the prolific writings of Luisa Piccarreta, has blossomed not merely in theological circles but also within the tender fibers of our communities. This divine revelation granted to Luisa has surged forth, igniting a fervor for living according to God's plan and reinforcing the unity among the faithful.

Consider first the transformation of local parishes. These bastions of faith, by embracing the teachings contained within the Book of Heaven, have seen a marked revival in spiritual engagement. Priests report more fervent participation in Mass, Confession, and adoration. Laypersons, inspired by the vibrancy of Divine Will, regularly come together to pray and discern, each gathering imbuing the participants with newfound vigor.

One cannot underestimate the familial rejuvenation wrought by these holy teachings. Households steeped in the Divine Will find themselves enveloped in an atmosphere of love and understanding, oftentimes breaking cycles of strife and discord. Husbands and wives, parents and children, bound together by an intentional desire to manifest God's Will in their daily lives, celebrate fruits of divine empathy and mutual respect. This emboldens each family, reinforcing the structure that indeed the family is the domestic church.

Moreover, as individuals immerse themselves in the teachings, an effusion of acts of charity becomes evident. Communities endowed with the awakening knowledge of Divine Will witness unparalleled generosity and selflessness. These are not mere acts of pity, but rather, genuine reflections of divine love—an extension of Christ's own compassion. Food drives, care for the elderly, support for the downtrodden, and educational initiatives are but a few manifestations of this collective transformation.

Educational institutions, too, have felt the embrace of the Divine Will. Schools under the auspices of the Church, once concerned primarily with academic and moral instruction, now find themselves deeply enriched with an added dimension of spiritual enlightenment. Students, from the earliest age, are imbued with principles of God's will, guiding their thoughts and actions to mirror heavenly virtues. Such an education fosters future generations who are not only well-versed in secular knowledge but are also steadfast in their faith.

This revelation's reach extends even to our youth. In an age often marred by confusion and moral ambivalence, the Divine Will Movement supplies a beacon of clarity. Youth groups and young adult ministries flourish as burgeoning believers find common ground in their ardent pursuit of God's will. Gatherings, retreats, and mission trips become crucibles of faith, forging bonds of brotherhood and sisterhood that transcend mere social connections, elevating them to spiritual kinship.

Communities have further been fortified by small groups or cenacles dedicated to studying the Book of Heaven. These intimate assemblies of believers delve deeply into the revelations given to Luisa, fostering a profound comprehension of divine truths. Each meeting, an intermingling of prayer, fellowship, and shared insight, becomes a sanctified occasion for mutual edification and communal growth. From these small seeds, larger fruit-bearing trees arise, their roots intertwined, nourishing the entire congregation.

Churches worldwide, inspired by the tenets of Divine Will, often engage in outreach that transcends parish boundaries. Collaboration among various parishes and dioceses engenders a broader sense of unity within the universal Church. Conferences, seminars, and workshops become the fertile ground for sowing seeds of understanding and mutual support, fostering a collective ascent towards living in the divine will.

Indeed, the Divine Will Movement has bridged gaps, not just within our communities, but beyond them. The spirit of ecumenism flourishes as other Christian sisters and brothers find resonance in the truths articulated by Luisa Piccarreta. The shared quest for divine understanding opens doors to dialogue, cooperation, and joint prayer initiatives, leading to a more profound unity amongst all who proclaim Christ.

The fruits also manifest in the digital sphere, where believers partake in forums and webinars, exchanging ideas and experiences that amplify their collective wisdom. These virtual communities, unconstrained by geographical boundaries, testify to the universal applicability and appeal of the Divine Will. These devoted pilgrims of the digital age, by sharing and supporting one another, transcend temporal limitations, building a global ecclesial body in harmony with God's will.

Additionally, there is a visible transformation within the individual believers themselves. Souls who immerse in the Divine Will teachings often report profound personal conversions. These transformations testify not just in grand gestures but in the quiet, steadfast faithfulness of daily life. Morning offerings, acts of surrender to the Divine Will, and even routine tasks become sanctified acts of worship.

Moreover, the movement has renewed the very understanding of sanctity. In a modern age rife with secularism, it presents a compelling narrative that sanctity is not relegated to the cloister but is attainable in the very heart of ordinary life. Thus, doctors, teachers, tradespeople, and homemakers alike find in their daily labor a calling to holiness, irrespective of their external circumstances.

Testimonies abound from across the globe. Stories of lives altered, healings - both physical and spiritual, and renewed vocations illustrate the tangible impacts of embracing the Divine Will. These testimonies serve not merely as anecdotes but as robust affirmations that the teachings encapsulated in the Book of Heaven are as potent today as they were at their revelation.

In conclusion, the fruits of the Divine Will Movement are not confined to the esoteric or the spiritual elite. They permeate every stratum of Catholic life, from the individual to the collective, from the local parish to the global Church. This very movement becomes an embodiment of the prayer, "Thy kingdom come, Thy will be done on earth as it is in heaven," realized through the lives of countless faithful who bear witness to its transformative power. As hearts and communities align themselves ever more closely with God's holy will, the world is drawn nearer to the divine harmony intended by our Creator.

Chapter 20: Church's Recognition And Validation

In the annals of ecclesiastical history, the Church's recognition and validation of the Book of Heaven stand as testament to the divine truths it harbors and the sanctity within its pages. Astutely, the Magisterium has scrutinized and ultimately embraced the revelations given to Luisa Piccarreta, acknowledging them as a profound extension of sacred tradition. The ecclesiastical endorsement, a beacon of divine favor, illuminates the path for the faithful who seek to immerse themselves in the Divine Will. Clergy, with their scholarly acumen and spiritual discernment, have affixed their endorsements, weaving the Book of Heaven into the fabric of accepted theological study. This union of human comprehension with celestial wisdom orchestrates an epic odyssey for the soul, affirming that what is divinely revealed finds a rightful place within the hallowed halls of the Church, offering the faithful an unfaltering guide on their earthly pilgrimage towards eternal unity with the Divine.

Official Statements

The Church, ever vigilant in her duty to safeguard the faithful from error and lead them towards the sublime heights of sanctity, has not remained silent on the matter of the Divine Will as revealed to Luisa Piccarreta. The Holy See, through various pontifical actions and ecclesiastical dicasteries, has issued numerous statements validating and recognizing the importance of these revelations. Let us delve into the gravity and depth of this ecclesiastical endorsement.

The first significant endorsement arrived with the imprimatur and nihil obstat granted to Luisa's writings. These marks of ecclesiastical approval affirm that her works are free of doctrinal error and can, with conscientious mind, be read by the faithful. Indeed, this clear seal of approval resonates throughout the corridors of time, inviting the Church to drink from the fountains of Divine Will explicated in The Book of Heaven.

In the annals of Church history, few documents wield the authority of an imprimatur. This imprimatur was bestowed upon several volumes of Luisa's writings by Archbishop Joseph Leo and Archbishop Carlo Maria Capella in the early 20th century. These endorsements reflect a profound examination and affirmation by ecclesiastical authorities, ensuring theological coherence with the Magisterium of the Roman Catholic Church.

The Servant of God, Pope Pius X, known for his ardent pursuit of tradition and truth, granted a special blessing to Luisa Piccarreta herself and her work. This benediction underscores the heavenly significance seen by the pontiff, whose papacy was marked by a deep desire to lead the flock into deeper communion with God's will. Furthermore, Pope Pius XI and Pius XII echoed similar sentiments, revealing a continuous thread of papal recognition that intertwines with Luisa's mission on earth.

In more recent times, the cause for Luisa Piccarreta's beatification serves as a magnanimous testament to the Church's belief in the sanctity and divine revelation bestowed upon her. The Archbishop of Trani-Barletta-Bisceglie-Nazareth, as the postulator of her cause, has diligently worked to present her life and writings for scrutiny and veneration. This ongoing process, already conferred with the title of Servant of God by the Congregation for the Causes of Saints, aims to elevate her to the status of the blessed, and eventually, sainthood.

This cause has been rooted in extensive theological examination, historical documentation, and personal testimonials. The rigorous nature of this process ensures that every word written by Luisa remains in harmonious consonance with the doctrines of the Roman Catholic Church. It is a journey measured in not mere years but a fervent pursuit of divine truth and human sanctity.

The voice of laity and clergy alike resounds in unison when considering the Divine Will Movement. Synods and clergy gatherings across continents have explored the teachings encapsulated in The Book of Heaven, finding within its pages a robust theologic nor rooted in divine love and the perennial wisdom of Catholic tradition. Bishops and priests from varied dioceses have attested to the transformative impact the Divine Will has had on their ministries and personal spiritual lives.

Particularly noteworthy is the endorsement by the Bishop of Trani-Barletta-Bisceglie, who, acting as Luisa's local ordinary and custodian of her cause for canonization, has actively promoted her writings. This episcopal support underpins a sincere recognition of her doctrine's spiritual worth and fidelity to Church teachings.

Likewise, the Vatican's Sacred Congregation for the Doctrine of the Faith has examined and invariably approved various elements of Luisa's writings. This approval signifies that the content is not only free from doctrinal error but also contributes meaningfully to the spiritual edification of the faithful. Such high level ecclesiastical nods of acceptance are paramount in ensuring the teachings therein align with the Sacred Tradition and Holy Scriptures.

The Divine Will Movement, inspired by Luisa's writings, has flourished internationally with the Church's watchful guidance. Ecclesiastical leaders from numerous nations have established centers for the spiritual formation of the faithful in the Divine Will. These centers act as beacons, guiding souls to the heart of this divine calling, nurturing their spiritual growth with pastoral and sacramental care.

A beautiful example lies in the work of the Association Luisa Piccarreta, established under the auspices of the Diocese of Trani. This association thrives as a haven for those who seek to live out the teachings of The Book of Heaven, bedding its roots deeply in the soil of Church approval and guidance. Such institutions attest to the Church's recognition and earnest desire to integrate the Divine Will into the lives of the faithful.

The papal encyclicals and apostolic exhortations frequently emphasize an invitation to greater interior life and conformity to God's will, themes that resonate profoundly with Luisa's revelations. The Magisterium, through these documents, often echoes the call to holiness and the intimate union with the Divine Will, reinforcing the truths Luisa articulated with such luminous clarity in her writings.

Lastly, the great symphony of saints whose lives perpetually harmonize with the Divine Will stands as a testament to its authenticity. The Church recognizes Luisa's writings as aligning with the teachings of eminent saints whose lives embody the fullness of surrender to God's will. This celestial alignment underscores a universal call to sanctity that transcends time and belongs to the Church's perennial mission.

In conclusion, the ecclesiastical recognition and validation of Luisa Piccarreta's work, her writings' doctrinal clarity, and their impact on countless souls reveal the depth and gravity of the Church's endorsement. As we journey through the annals of history and the realm of human souls touched by The Book of Heaven, it is clear that these divine truths beckon us closer to the heart of God's infinite will. Such validation is not merely an ecclesiastical formality but a call to immerse ourselves wholly in the boundless ocean of Divine Will.

Endorsements By Clergy

As the Divine Will Movement burgeoned, it inevitably beckoned the discerning eyes of the Church's clergy who, steeped in tradition and wisdom, sought to validate its authenticity and divine origin. These endorsements by luminaries of our sacred Church are not mere formalities but bear witnesses to the spiritual profundity found within the "Book of Heaven" and the revelations imparted unto Luisa Piccarreta.

One must acknowledge the Bishop of Trani-Barletta-Bisceglie, Monsignor Giuseppe M. Leo, whose ecclesiastical authority deeply scrutinized Luisa's writings. His ardent dedication to theology did not lead to mere passive observations but to a wholehearted endorsement. Bishop Leo, understanding the importance of divine revelations in alignment with Sacred Tradition, provided a commendable validation, ensuring that the faithful could trust in the Divine Will Movement's theological soundness.

Intertwined with Bishop Leo's ecclesiastical endorsement was that of Archbishops and Cardinals, whose deep-rooted erudition and pastoral care steered them toward recognizing the fruits borne from Luisa's revelations. Cardinal Lavitrano of Palermo, renowned for his theological insight, earnestly encouraged the continued study and practice of the Divine Will teachings. His words echoed through the halls of the faithful, reinforcing the Movement's spiritual legitimacy.

Each endorsement brings a layer of ecclesial credibility, echoing from the Vatican to parishes worldwide. The recognition by clergy extends beyond mere approval but stands as a testament to the meticulously examined spiritual revelations Luisa shared. Few understand this better than Archbishop Cassati, who, having examined the volumes with scrupulous attention, also pronounced favorably. His commendation served as a linchpin, drawing together various threads of theological discourse into a coherent validation.

It is noteworthy to mention the profound words of Monsignor Paolo Rizzi, Postulator for the Cause of Canonization of Luisa Piccarreta, who encapsulated the essence of these endorsements with utmost eloquence. "Luisa's writings," Monsignor Rizzi articulated, "resonate with the fruits of divine inspiration, mirrored in the lives of the countless souls transformed by the Divine Will teachings." Such venerated utterances bridge the gap between ancient theological understanding and contemporary spiritual practice.

Among the myriad voices, one cannot overlook the pivotal role of Father Bernardino Giuseppe Bucci, OFM, whose familiarity with Luisa herself endowed him with a unique perspective. Father Bucci's lived experiences and spiritual encounters with Luisa invigorated his endorsements with a personal touch, providing invaluable insights that enriched the fabric of the Church's recognition.

Indeed, Father Bucci's endorsements harmonize with those of other clergy whose personal encounters and spiritual discernments lead them to vouch for the Divine Will's authenticity. Consider the profound testament of Monsignor J.L. Picard, who described Luisa's writings as "a luminous testament to divine intimacy, guiding the faithful towards a deeper union with God's Will." Such expressions, derived from prayerful consideration, reflect the profound impact that Luisa's revelations have etched upon the hearts of the clergy.

Endorsements have not only come from individual clergies but from ecclesiastical bodies as well, weaving a complex tapestry of collective validation for the Divine Will Movement. Diocesan inquiries, often rigorous in their pursuit of doctrinal purity, have yielded in favor of Luisa's revelations, emphasizing their consonance with Catholic doctrine and their potential to foster spiritual growth among the faithful.

The Holy Office, the Church's guardian of doctrine, examined Luisa's volumes with perspicacity, ensuring their theological integrity before offering imprimatur. This stamp bears significant weight, conveying that the "Book of Heaven" aligns with the magisterium and does not deviate from the tenets of our faith. Such affirmations are indispensable, providing a bulwark against misinterpretations and theological deviations.

Furthermore, the role of religious orders in endorsing the Divine Will Movement cannot be understated. The Servants of God, often vanguards of spiritual renewal, found in Luisa's revelations an inexhaustible wellspring of divine wisdom. Priests and theologians within these orders, steeped in contemplative prayer and scholarly study, have provided heartfelt endorsements, reinforcing the significance of living in the Divine Will.

It is also pivotal to appreciate the commendations from global perspectives. Clergy from diverse cultural milieus and ecclesiastical traditions have found unity in their endorsements of Luisa's work. African bishops, Latin American cardinals, and Asian patriarchs have all converged in a harmonious chorus, extolling the virtues of the Divine Will teachings and recognizing their universal applicability.

The presence of these endorsements creates an environment of trust and reverence around the Book of Heaven, encouraging the laity to delve deeper into its mysteries. Each clergy who has endorsed Luisa's revelations serves as a mediator, enabling the faithful to approach the Divine Will with confidence and joy. This ecclesiastical matrimony of spiritual insight and doctrinal approval paves the path for a robust spiritual journey for those who seek to live in the Divine Will.

In conclusion, the endorsements by the clergy, infused with theological acumen and spiritual ardor, stand as pillars supporting the edifice of the Divine Will Movement. Their collective recognition accentuates that the revelations imparted unto Luisa Piccarreta are not only a celestial beacon but align quintessentially with the tenants of Holy Mother Church. These endorsements serve as both guide and reassurance, allowing the faithful to navigate the profound depths of Divine Will teachings with unwavering faith and divine inspiration.

Chapter 21: Scholarly Analysis Of The Book Of Heaven

In embarking upon a scholarly analysis of "The Book of Heaven," one must delve deeply into the multi-faceted theological insights that this sacred text offers. The very essence of Luisa Piccarreta's revelations, like threads woven into the grand tapestry of Divine Will, provide an unparalleled lens into the supernatural plan of God. Scholars have fervently pored over these volumes, uncovering layers of divine wisdom that align so harmoniously with Roman Catholic doctrine. Academic studies have unveiled the profound and meticulous nature of these revelations, illuminating the intricate relationship between human free will and Divine Providence. The fruits of these labors have been twofold: not only have they affirmed the legitimacy of the Divine Will Movement, but they have also enriched the spiritual lives of countless believers. Thus, the "Book of Heaven" stands robust as a divinely revealed masterpiece, offering inexhaustible wells of spiritual nourishment and fortifying the faithful in their journey towards eternal sanctity.

Theological Insights

The theological foundation of the "Book of Heaven," penned by Luisa Piccarreta, offers a cavernous depth of spiritual wisdom and insight that remains an aventine abbey of divine mysteries. Central to its core is the doctrine of Living in the Divine Will, a teaching that aligns harmoniously with the sacred traditions of our Holy Church. This doctrine propounds an intimate participation in the very life of God, beckoning believers to subsume their human will into the Divine Will, thus enabling the operation of God's Will within the mundane aspects of daily life. Of note is the correlation between the sanctifying grace offered through the sacraments and this transcendental embodiment of Divine Will, uncovering a seamless tapestry strewn with theological fabric.

The "Book of Heaven" elucidates the nature of God's immensity and omnipresence, proclaiming that all of creation is continuously imbued with His divine essence. Such conceptualization challenges the devotee to perceive a constant divine confluence within the natural realm. This perspective compels one to a deeper understanding of the sacramental principle that the outward, visible signs of grace are indeed reflections of divine inward realities. The theological resonance is much akin to the Scriptural affirmations found in the Psalms, asserting, "The earth is full of the goodness of the Lord" (Psalm 33:5).

Furthermore, one could find parallels in the ancient writings of the Desert Fathers and Mothers, who sought the solitary abode to immerse themselves wholly in God's presence. The "Book of Heaven" and their ascetic endeavors share a common pursuit—the unity with the Divine Will. This aspiration towards divinisation or "theosis" underscores our call to transform our human conditions through the sanctification of God, reminiscent of Saint Athanasius's proclamation, "God became man so that man might become god." It subtly reiterates that such union with God's will is the ultimate destiny for the human soul.

Additionally, Luisa's revelations provide a theological critique and enhancement of the understanding of original sin and its repercussions on human will. It elucidates how the redemption wrought by Christ not only heals but elevates humanity, enabling a return to prelapsarian grace. By synchronizing one's will with the Divine Will, believers can potentially restore the lost harmony that was once enjoyed by Adam in Eden. This is akin to Saint Paul's discourse in Romans 5:19, "For just as through the disobedience of the one man the many were made sinners, so also through the obedience of the one man the many will be made righteous."

Luisa offers a profound exposition on the role and dignity of Mary, the Most Holy Virgin. As the perfect model of living in the Divine Will, Mary is extolled as the new Eve, whose "fiat" inaugurates a new creation. Her profound obedience becomes a luminous exemplar for believers, guiding them to attune their heartstrings to the symphony of God's will. This Mariological dimension enhances the theological landscape, reinforcing the universality and depth of this sacred admonition, resonant with the Church's magisterial teachings.

Moreover, the "Book of Heaven" propounds a dynamic and evolving understanding of sanctification. It posits that living in the Divine Will is not a static state but an ever-deepening spiral into divine intimacy. This dynamic process is reminiscent of Saint John of the Cross's mystical theology, suggesting a continual ascent towards the Divine through the purgative, illuminative, and unitive ways. It is an invitation to perpetual transformation and elevation, seeking to attain higher degrees of divine likeness.

This book elucidates the interconnectedness of the human soul with all of creation, invoking Saint Francis of Assisi's Canticle of the Creatures. It fosters a theological ecology, recognizing creation as an opus of Divine Will. This perspective provides a fresh vantage point on environmental stewardship, underscoring that care for creation mirrors allegiance to God's will. Thus, the call to divine obedience also becomes a clarion call to eco-responsibility, echoing the encyclicals such as "Laudato Si'."

Another pivotal theological aspect is the adoption of the Divine Will as a means to sanctify and redeem human suffering. Lucidly, this aligns with Pope John Paul II's theology of redemptive suffering found in "Salvifici Doloris." Luisa intimates that through union with the Divine Will, one's sufferings partake in Christ's salvific mission, becoming a conduit of grace not only for oneself but also for the entire world. This embodies a cosmic dimension, encouraging a participatory engagement in the redemption of all creation.

To delve deeper into its theological profundity, consider the Eucharistic dimensions found within the "Book of Heaven." The sacrament is portrayed not merely as a memorial but as an active perpetuation of God's Will made manifest. This Eucharistic theology thereby invites the faithful to a more profound adoration and transformative participation. The very act of receiving the Eucharist becomes a mutual indwelling, a sacred fusion of wills, reminiscent of Saint Augustine's words, "Become what you receive."

The "Book of Heaven" also offers a theological anthropology that magnifies the dignity and purpose of the human soul. It articulates the notion that humanity is designed for divine collaboration, echoing Saint Thomas Aquinas's assertion that grace does not destroy nature but perfects it. This theology affirms that the act of living in the Divine Will actualizes our ultimate purpose, a theme that reverberates with the Church's teachings on vocation and calling.

Thus, the theological dimensions of the "Book of Heaven" forge a comprehensive framework that harmonizes with sacred tradition, augmenting it with fresh perspectives. As the faithful immerse themselves in its rich narratives, they are invited into a deeper understanding of divine mysteries. Far from being an isolated revelation, it operates synergistically within the magisterium of the Church, amplifying the song of salvation history.

Distinctly, the theological insights drawn from this sacred text speak to the universal call to holiness. They beckon the laity and the clergy alike to a fuller, richer life in God's divine orchestration. In the harmonic convergence of divine and human wills, the Church finds her true song, her raison d'être, her participation in the eternal liturgy of heaven.

Academic Studies

The academic examination of "The Book of Heaven" unveils layers of theological depth that not only fortify the faith of believers but also provide fertile ground for scholarly discourse. Within this realm, scholars meticulously analyze the Scriptural and doctrinal congruence of the Divine Will teachings as imparted to Luisa Piccarreta. The convergence of mysticism and orthodoxy in Luisa's revelations presents a compelling case for an intense scholarly scrutiny to affirm the Divine origins of her writings.

Scholars have approached "The Book of Heaven" with a keen eye for theological consistency and doctrinal soundness. Their inquiries delve into the essence of God's plan, as laid out in the teachings of the Divine Will. Here, they juxtapose Luisa's accounts with established Church doctrine to ascertain the authenticity and alignment of her revelations with the broader corpus of Catholic theology. This methodical approach not only validates the theological insights found within "The Book of Heaven" but also elucidates their significance to contemporary Catholic spirituality.

Through rigorous exegeses, scholars discern that the writings of Luisa Piccarreta unveil profound understandings of divine operations and human cooperation with the Divine Will. Her texts, deeply rooted in traditional Catholic mysticism, draw parallels with the works of great saints and mystics. The scholarly endeavor to situate Luisa's revelations within this historical context underscores the continuity of her insights with the mystical traditions endorsed by the Church.

An important dimension of academic studies on "The Book of Heaven" involves historical-critical analyses. Researchers explore the socio-historical context of Luisa's life, her socio-political environment, and how these factors influenced her mystical experiences. This comprehensive investigation helps to frame her revelations within the vicissitudes of her time, providing a richer understanding of their reception and implications.

Moreover, comparative analyses with other saints and mystics constitute a significant aspect of academic studies on the Book of Heaven. By juxtaposing Luisa's teachings with those of St. Teresa of Avila, St. John of the Cross, and others, scholars illuminate both the unique and the universal elements of her mystical insights. Such comparisons elevate her texts within the canon of Christian mysticism and demonstrate the perennial nature of Divine truths.

Another critical area of scholarly inquiry is in the field of systematic theology. Here, theologians grapple with the intricate details of Luisa's explications on the Divine Will, exploring the ontological and epistemological dimensions of her revelations. This systematic approach helps clarify the complex theological constructs inherent in her writings, making them more accessible to the faithful and enriching the theoretical foundations of Catholic theology.

In the realm of moral theology, scholars examine the ethical implications of living in the Divine Will as prescribed in "The Book of Heaven." By dissecting Luisa's exhortations on virtue, charity, and sanctification, researchers provide practical frameworks for believers seeking to incorporate these teachings into their daily lives. Such analyses underscore the transformative potential of Luisa's revelations, showcasing their capacity to elevate ordinary lives to extraordinary sanctity.

The dialogue between academics and ecclesiastical authorities is another vital element in the scholarly study of "The Book of Heaven." Through symposia, conferences, and workshops, theologians and clergy engage in robust discussions to elucidate and disseminate the profound wisdom contained in Luisa's writings. This collaborative approach not only fosters a deeper understanding of the Divine Will but also ensures that these teachings are effectively integrated within the broader theological landscape of the Church.

Scholars have also dedicated themselves to textual criticism of "The Book of Heaven." By analyzing the original manuscripts, they strive to preserve the integrity of Luisa's writings, ensuring that translations and interpretations remain faithful to her original expressions. This meticulous scholarship guarantees that the theological riches embedded in her texts are transmitted accurately to future generations.

Furthermore, interdisciplinary studies have emerged as a fruitful area of academic inquiry. Specialists in psychology, sociology, and even natural sciences have started to explore the influence of the Divine Will teachings on human behavior, community dynamics, and personal well-being. These interdisciplinary efforts broaden the scope of Luisa's revelations, demonstrating their relevance not only within theological circles but also in the broader realm of human knowledge and activity.

In light of the growing body of academic work on "The Book of Heaven," it becomes evident that these revelations serve as a wellspring of divine wisdom, capable of nourishing both the intellect and the spirit. Scholars, by engaging deeply with Luisa's mystical insights, contribute significantly to the ongoing theological and spiritual renewal within the Church. Their rigorous analyses and thoughtful expositions affirm the divinely inspired nature of "The Book of Heaven," fortifying the faith of believers and enriching the tapestry of Catholic theology for generations to come.

Chapter 22: Defending The Divine Will Movement

As the tendrils of time entwine around the faithful, it is paramount to shield the Divine Will Movement from the shadows of scepticism. In contemplation of the luminous revelations bequeathed unto Luisa Piccarreta, we find an irrefutable consonance with the Sacred Tradition, thus dissolving the mists of doubt. The foundations laid within the "Book of Heaven" bear testament to the celestial whisperings, inviting the devout into a sanctified dance with the Divine Will. Critics may arise, brandishing their quills dipped in incredulity, yet their parchment shan't comprehend the ethereal trust inscribed in hearts aflame with divine love. Let us, thus, not falter but rather gird our loins, elucidating the harmony betwixt revealed truths and apostolic teachings. By so doing, we not only enkindle the candles of understanding but also fortify the citadel of faith against the tempests of misconception. This movement, a testament to divine arbitration, stands as a beacon, drawing us ever closer to His merciful embrace.

Responding To Critics

The Divine Will Movement has not escaped the gaze of skeptics and critics who question its legitimacy, its origins, and its theological soundness. These criticisms, often arising from a misunderstanding or a lack of in-depth study, require a measured and thoughtful response grounded in both faith and reason. These detractors frequently overlook the profound spiritual insights and the alignment with Sacred Tradition that the Divine Will teachings uphold.

To address these critiques, we must first clarify the nature of private revelations within the Catholic Church. The Church, while upholding the primacy of public revelation contained in Scripture and Tradition, recognizes that private revelations can offer valuable spiritual insights. The revelations given to Luisa Piccarreta, as documented in the "Book of Heaven," should be viewed within this context. The Church's caution in officially recognizing private revelations should not be misconstrued as a negation of their potential value.

Critics often assert that the Divine Will teachings deviate from established Church doctrines. However, upon closer examination, the messages received by Luisa Piccarreta remain firmly anchored in the grand tapestry of Catholic theology. These teachings emphasize a profound union with God, echoing the aspirations of many saints who sought to live entirely according to God's will. The essence of living in the Divine Will is not a heretic innovation but rather a deepened understanding of the desired intimacy between the Creator and His creation.

Moreover, some argue that the concepts articulated in the Book of Heaven are too novel and not explicitly found in earlier theological works. Yet, the Church's history is replete with mystics and theologians who introduced new depths of understanding. Saint Thomas Aquinas, Saint John of the Cross, and Saint Teresa of Avila each added layers to the Church's spiritual heritage without negating prior truths. Similarly, the revelations to Luisa enrich our comprehension of divine love and human sanctification without contradicting foundational doctrines.

Another point of contention revolves around Luisa Piccarreta's spiritual experiences. Skeptics question the authenticity of her visions and locutions, suggesting that they could be products of fervent imagination or psychological anomalies. It is essential to note that the Church has historically approached mystical experiences with caution, employing rigorous discernment processes. Luisa's writings and the testimonies of those who knew her provide compelling evidence of her sanctity and the supernatural nature of her experiences. Her life of virtue, humility, and obedience to the Church further bolster the credibility of her revelations.

Additionally, the accusations that the Divine Will Movement promotes passivity or quietism are unfounded. Critics misinterpret the call to live in the Divine Will as an invitation to idleness. On the contrary, those who embrace this calling are summoned to an active participation in God's creative and redemptive work. Their actions, though hidden, become imbued with divine efficacy, mirroring the hidden life of Christ at Nazareth. By living in the Divine Will, believers engage in a dynamic and transformative journey that demands a continual surrender and active cooperation with divine grace.

Matters of doctrinal orthodoxy are frequently raised in opposition to the Divine Will Movement. Yet, the extensive examination by several theologians and ecclesiastical authorities attests to its alignment with the core teachings of the Church. Moreover, the movement does not claim superiority to the teachings of Christ but invites a deeper immersion into the mysteries of faith. It echoes the call to holiness present in the Gospel, urging the faithful to embody the prayer "Thy will be done on earth as it is in Heaven," in every facet of their lives.

A common misconception is that the Divine Will Movement seeks to supplant traditional devotions and established spiritual practices. This is a significant misinterpretation. Rather than replacing these time-honored devotions, the Divine Will teachings aim to infuse them with a more profound dedication to God's will. Whether through the Rosary, Eucharistic adoration, or acts of charity, every devotional practice can be elevated by the intention of living fully in accordance with the Divine Will.

It is also necessary to address the critique concerning the spread and promotion of the Divine Will Movement. Detractors may argue that its recent growth and enthusiastic following hint at a kind of spiritual sensationalism. However, history has shown that genuine spiritual movements often arise in times of particular need. The burgeoning interest in the Divine Will Movement can be interpreted as a response to the contemporary longing for deeper spiritual fulfillment and divine intimacy, rather than an ephemeral trend.

An important measure of any spiritual movement's authenticity is its fruits. The Divine Will Movement has produced numerous testimonies of personal transformation, increased devotion, and a discernible impact on communities. These positive outcomes are indicative of its divine origins and constructive influence. By their fruits, we shall know them; and the fruits of the Divine Will Movement have been overwhelmingly positive, fostering virtue and deepening faith

.

In sum, responding to critics of the Divine Will Movement necessitates a thorough and nuanced approach. It calls for a reaffirmation of the movement's doctrinal fidelity, an explanation of its theological underpinnings, and a presentation of the tangible spiritual fruits it has produced. Addressing misconceptions and misunderstandings with patience and clarity will pave the way for a broader acceptance and appreciation of the profound spiritual treasures that the Divine Will teachings offer to the Church and the world.

Promoting Understanding

In the grand tapestry that we weave herein to defend the Divine Will Movement, it becomes abundantly paramount to foster understanding amongst the faithful. The mission lies not in the mere exclamation of beliefs but in a deeper, resonant enlightenment that stirs the heart and fortifies the spirit. Promoting understanding stands as both a beacon and bulwark, guiding souls towards the light of truth and dispelling the shadows of doubt. Is it not the sacred duty of believers to delve into the wellsprings of divine wisdom, patiently uncovering the hidden gems bestowed by Luisa Piccarreta?

To commence, one must recognize the manifold layers of the Book of Heaven. It is a tome of celestial dialogues, of profound divine revelations, akin to the whisperings of angels captured upon the parchment. The heart of understanding the Divine Will Movement pulsates within these sacred pages. Christ Himself, through His revered disciple Luisa, bestowed insights not merely as commands but as invitations. Invitations to partake in the divine, to unite the human will with the divine, creating a harmonious existence rooted in God's ultimate plan. Is this not a call worthy of our attention and devotion?

"Thy will be done, on earth as it is in heaven" is the sacred prayer offered by our Lord, and herein lies the crux of promoting understanding. It is not an abstract concept but a lived reality. To comprehend fully, one must approach with an open heart, unburdened by preconceptions. The practice of living in the Divine Will is not reserved for the mystics or the holy alone; it beckons all who seek unity with the Creator. Therefore, elucidating these teachings with clarity and compassion is indispensable for nurturing a robust faith community.

Promoting understanding also involves dismantling erroneous notions that may cloud vision. Some may erroneously perceive the Divine Will Movement as a deviation or an undue complexity added to the simplicity of faith. Quite the contrary, it is an extension of orthodoxy, deeply entwined with the sacred tradition and magisterium of the Church. In confronting such misapprehensions, it is essential to reference the scriptural foundations laid out in the Word of God, as well as endorsements from saints and theologians who found resonance in Luisa's divine encounters.

We must recall the nature of divine pedagogy. The Lord imparts wisdom progressively, akin to a master artist revealing a grand masterpiece stroke by stroke. The volumes of the Book of Heaven are such an unveiling. Promoting understanding demands patient exposition, whereby each volume is seen not in isolation but as part of a cohesive and divine narrative. Herein, we realize the import of summarizing and distilling key themes and revelations, emphasizing their interconnectedness within the grand schema of redemption and sanctification.

In the pursuit of promoting understanding, it is imperative to engage the intellect and the spirit harmoniously. Faith and reason are twin pillars that support the edifice of divine truth. Through scholarly exegesis and heartfelt testimonies, we present a holistic view of the Divine Will Movement. Academic studies, theological inquiries, and pastoral reflections meld to create a comprehensive picture that illuminates minds and enkindles hearts. Furthermore, testimonies of transformation and living faith serve as both validation and inspiration, breathing life into doctrinal principles.

One must consider the vast historical and spiritual lineage from which the Divine Will Movement springs forth. By situating Luisa Piccarreta's revelations within the broader context of Church history, we foster a more profound appreciation and understanding. Just as the Church Fathers and Doctors illuminated the path of faith in their times, so do Luisa's writings serve as a guiding light in our contemporary era. Promoting understanding, therefore, encompasses a symbiotic relationship between the new and the old, synthesizing them to reveal greater truths.

Moreover, the role of pastoral guidance cannot be overstressed. Shepherds of the flock, our priests and bishops, are pivotal in interpreting and disseminating these divine teachings. Their endorsement and elucidation lend credence and provide the necessary pastoral care to incorporate such teachings into the daily lives of the faithful. It behooves us, therefore, to support and educate our clergy, ensuring they are well-versed in the profound spiritual riches offered by the Divine Will Movement.

The journey towards a deepened understanding is a collective one. It requires communal engagement, where dialogues and discussions foster an environment of mutual growth and enlightenment. Study groups, seminars, and catechetical programs centered on the Book of Heaven can significantly enhance comprehension and practical application. This communal approach ensures that the teachings are not merely theoretical but lived and experienced within the Christian community, thereby bearing visible and lasting fruit.

Promoting understanding, in its truest essence, is an act of charity. It is the compassionate endeavor to share the divine wisdom generously bestowed upon us. Through catechesis, homilies, and spiritual direction, we extend an invitation to all souls to immerse themselves in the divine mysteries and live in the tranquility of God's will. This work of enlightenment is thus a ministry, a sacred service to our brethren, guiding them towards the ineffable joy of living in union with the Divine Will.

In conclusion, promoting understanding within the context of the Divine Will Movement requires a dedicated and multifaceted approach. It calls for clarity, compassion, and commitment, ensuring that the profound teachings and revelations of Luisa Piccarreta are both accessible and transformative. By embracing this mission, we do more than defend; we awaken the faithful to a deeper and more harmonious relationship with the Divine, fostering a community that truly lives and breathes the sacred Will of God.

Chapter 23: Implementing The Divine Will In Daily Life

As one embarks upon the sacred endeavor of living in accord with the Divine Will, the essence of daily life transforms into a magnificent tapestry woven with divine threads. Each moment becomes an opportunity to transcend the earthly and embrace the heavenly, to act not from the self but from the profound depths of God's eternal will. The call to "fiat" echoes through the ordinary tasks of our day, inviting us to sanctify our actions and imbue them with celestial significance. Emulating the humble obedience of Luisa Piccarreta, we find that every breath, every gesture, and every word can reflect the splendor of divine harmony. Hence, it is through our steadfast commitment to aligning with the Divine Will that we uncover a sanctified existence, where the mundane metamorphoses into a realm of spiritual communion, fostering an unwavering testament to the boundless grace bestowed upon us by the Almighty.

Practical Steps

Embarking upon the path of aligning one's life with the Divine Will requires both fervent desire and practical application. The grandeur of such a calling may seem daunting; yet, it is through humble, daily acts that one can ascend to the celestial heights intended by our Heavenly Father. By weaving the Divine Will into the very fabric of our daily existence, we begin to emulate a life of sanctity, guided by celestial light.

First and foremost, the discipline of daily prayer is indispensable. To live in the Divine Will, one must be anchored in constant communion with God. Begin your day with a heartfelt offering of all actions, thoughts, and words to align with His will. The morning prayer serves as a cornerstone, setting the tone for the entire day. Without this foundational act, our endeavors may lack divine direction.

Furthermore, partake in the Holy Sacraments as frequently as possible. The Holy Eucharist, in particular, becomes the sustenance for living in the Divine Will. When we receive the Body and Blood of Christ, we are not merely fulfilling a ritual but infusing ourselves with divine grace that strengthens our union with God's will. Participating in the sacrament of Reconciliation regularly allows us to cleanse our souls and realign ourselves with the divine path.

The reading of 'The Book of Heaven' should become a daily practice. In these voluminous writings, dictated by Jesus to Luisa Piccarreta, we find the divine instructions that are to shape our existence. Make it a habit to meditate on a passage each day, contemplating its application in your life. This daily reflection can serve as a compass, guiding you towards actions that are in harmony with God's Will.

Moreover, living in the Divine Will is not merely a matter of grand gestures but rather is found in the simplicity of daily tasks. Perform even the most mundane chores with a spirit of love and offering. Whether you are cooking, cleaning, or working, do everything for the glory of God. Transform these ordinary moments into acts of divine love, consciously inviting God's Will into every part of your life.

Kindness and charity towards others are practical manifestations of the Divine Will. Jesus implores us to love our neighbors as ourselves. Start by lending a helping hand to those in need, listening with empathy to someone in distress, or simply offering a smile. These small acts of love ripple through the universe, echoing divine harmony and goodness.

Another vital step is to cultivate interior silence and acceptance. In our bustling, modern lives, finding moments of quiet can be challenging, yet it is in this silence that we can hear the whisper of God's Will. Take time for silent prayer, meditation, or adoration before the Blessed Sacrament. In these moments of stillness, we can find clarity and guidance from the Holy Spirit.

Be prepared to face trials and tribulations, for living in the Divine Will does not exempt one from life's adversities. These challenges are, in fact, divine opportunities to grow in virtue and reliance upon God. When hardships arise, offer them as sacrifices to God, trusting in His greater plan. This surrender, though difficult, purifies our wills and strengthens our resolve to remain faithful.

Integrate spiritual readings and teachings into your daily routine. The wisdom of saints, Church Fathers, and contemporary Catholic writers can provide insight and motivation as you endeavor to live in the Divine Will. These readings can serve as spiritual nourishment, continually guiding and correcting our path.

It's essential to involve your family or community in this journey. Sharing insights and experiences with others can create a supportive environment where the Divine Will is collectively sought and cherished. Organize study groups, family prayers, or community service projects that align with divine teachings. Together, your lives can form a tapestry of grace and service.

In the hustle of daily life, make frequent spiritual retreats, if possible. These can be days spent in a monastery, a day of silence in a park, or even an afternoon in uninterrupted prayer at home. Such retreats allow for a deeper immersion into the Divine Will, providing the soul with the rest and focus needed to return to daily life with renewed vigor.

Another step is to actively combat any vices and cultivate virtues. Identify areas in your life where sin may have a foothold and work diligently to uproot them. Seek divine assistance through prayer, and engage in acts of penance and self-discipline. Concurrently, strive to cultivate virtues such as patience, humility, and charity. Each virtue you develop brings you closer to living in harmony with the Divine Will.

Engage frequently in acts of thanksgiving. Recognize the blessings that you receive daily, and express your gratitude to God. This practice of thanksgiving not only enriches your spiritual life but also aligns you more closely with the Divine Will as you develop a heart that is perpetually turned towards God's goodness.

Finally, seek guidance from a spiritual director who understands the teachings of the Divine Will. A knowledgeable director can provide personalized advice, encouragement, and correction, helping you stay on the path toward divine union. This mentorship can be priceless, offering clarity and support as you navigate the complexities of living in God's Will.

In conclusion, implementing the Divine Will in daily life is an ongoing journey, marked by intentional acts of prayer, service, and spiritual growth. Embrace each day as an opportunity to align more deeply with God's Will, and trust that in these consistent, humble steps, you are contributing to the unfolding of His divine plan.

Success Stories

Thus, from the heart of the Divine Will Movement emerge a cornucopia of tales, resplendent in their simplicity and profound in their divine orchestration, attesting to the efficacy of implementing the Divine Will in daily life. Each narrative, a beacon of transformative grace, serves as a testament to the extraordinary fruits borne by those who surrender to the Infinite Love and Wisdom of the Divine.

Consider, for instance, the life of Seraphina, a humble woman from a modest village. Her days were entwined with the toils of everyday existence, yet imbued with an unwavering commitment to embracing the Divine Will. Through her devotion to the teachings of Luisa Piccarreta, she discovered a fount of serenity amidst life's tumult. The divine simplicity in her countenance reflected a soul enkindled by the Holy Spirit. Her once strenuous labor became an offering, a prayerful act perpetually united with the Will of God. Seraphina's story has inspired many within her community to seek higher spiritual aspirations, thus binding their hearts in the willingness to embrace God's grand design.

In another realm, we find the tale of Brother Raphael, a man of faith laboring in the vineyard of ecclesial service. He erected his life as an altar, perpetually seeking to live in the Divine Will. His fervent engagement with the volumes of the Book of Heaven graced him with insights that illuminated his spiritual path. His homilies, once conventional, burgeoned into profound reflections animated by his communion with the Divine. Parishioners, young and old, flocked to his sermons, eager to sip from the wellsprings of Divine Wisdom he so generously shared. His parish transformed into a beacon of divine radiance, nurturing a community bound by the threads of God's Will.

Then there is the saga of young Beatrice, a soul bathed in the light of divine inspiration. From her earliest days, the writings of Luisa Piccarreta were her guiding stars. Though beset with trials distinctive of youthful ventures, she embraced the Divine Will with a fervor that set her apart. Her every action became a testament to the love she bore for Christ. Her peers, captivated by her unwavering joy and peace, sought the secret to her radiant spirit. She became a conduit, guiding hearts, both near and far, to the embrace of the Divine Will. Her witness speaks volumes on the transformative power of divine love and aligns beautifully with the grand tapestry of God's Eternal Plan.

Not to be forgotten is the epic of Father Ignatius, whose life exemplifies an ardent devotion to merging Divine Will with pastoral care. Amidst the labyrinth of ministerial duties, he found solace and strength in the words of Luisa Piccarreta. His prayers, sermons, and even mundane tasks transformed into offerings imbued with divine grace. The Divine Will animated his life, rendering every act a hymn of praise. His parish thrived under this divine guidance, nurturing vocations, fostering deeper faith, and forming a community enkindled by the Holy Spirit.

Countless such stories emanate from the heartbeat of this divine movement. They form a constellation of living testaments that shine brightly in the firmament of faith. Each tale, unique in its essence yet united in its divine purpose, bears witness to the boundless grace bestowed upon those who fervently embrace the Divine Will. The transformation wrought in lives both ordinary and extraordinary serves as an inspiring herald, calling the faithful to align their wills with the Eternal.

Moreover, the Divine Will Movement's impact on communities is worth noting. In suburban enclaves and bustling cities alike, the principles of the Divine Will have permeated the fabric of communal life. Prayer groups burgeon with enthusiasm, eager to delve deeper into the treasures of the Book of Heaven. Families, motivated by the teachings of Luisa Piccarreta, discover new depths of unity and love. Their homes, once ordinary dwellings, become sanctuaries of divine harmony where every action is a ripple in the ocean of God's Will.

In the broader ecclesial context, this divine alignment has stirred clergy and laypersons into spheres of renewed vigor. Bishops and priests, inspired by the transformative tales of those who live in the Divine Will, incorporate these teachings into their pastoral mission. Retreats and seminars devoted to exploring the depths of the Book of Heaven are met with overflowing attendance, indicative of the spiritual hunger that pervades the faithful. The Movement has fostered a resurgence of interest in the mystical union with God, a return to the sacredness of daily life imbued with divine intention.

Significantly, the movement has also prompted a renaissance in charitable acts and social justice. Inspired by the Divine Teachings, believers channel their faith into actions that uplift the marginalized and downtrodden. Acts of charity, wherein the face of Christ is seen in the least of our brethren, become frequent and fervent. Soup kitchens, orphanages, and shelters find new vigor and sustenance from those moved by divine inspiration. The Divine Will, thus, transcends the mystical and impels believers into the tangible realm of love and service.

This tapestry of grace and transformation continues to be woven by the myriad hands of those touched by the Divine Will. These success stories, resonant in their divine simplicity and profound impact, stand as luminous witnesses to the truth and efficacy of surrendering to God's Eternal Plan. They are not mere anecdotes but are the living stones with which the edifice of the Divine Will Movement is built.

As these stories attest, implementing the Divine Will in daily life does not require extraordinary circumstances but a surrendered heart. Through the eternal pages of the Book of Heaven, Luisa Piccarreta's revelations invite all to partake in this divine adventure, to transform the mundane into the holy, and to breathe the sacred into every fiber of their existence. This journey, embraced with humility and steadfast devotion, promises to yield fruits beyond the comprehension of mortal minds, beckoning the faithful to a life ensconced in divine grace.

In conclusion, the lives transfigured by the Divine Will underscore its timeless and universal applicability. From humble villagers to learned theologians, from cloistered hearts to bustling families, the eternal rhythm of the Divine Will echoes. It calls all to a higher destiny, a life lived not for the self, but for the divine glory. Such is the legacy of the Divine Will Movement – a testament to the heavens, a reflection of our Creator's Eternal Love, and an invitation to divine intimacy that transforms the very fabric of daily existence into a symphony of divine grace.

Chapter 24: Passing On The Teachings

In the sacred task of passing on the teachings of the Divine Will, one must wield the torch of celestial wisdom with grace and diligence. The apostles of this movement, adorned with the virtues of humility and perseverance, are called to illuminate the hearts of many, guiding them to the luminous truths revealed in the Book of Heaven. Methods of evangelization shall be manifold and creative, ensuring that each soul, regardless of its station, may drink from the eternal waters of divine knowledge. The scriptures, the Church's timeless wisdom, and the revelations granted to Luisa Piccarreta—all these serve as invaluable resources for education. By intertwining daily life with the divine precepts, believers can create a tapestry of faith so rich and profound that even the most hardened hearts shall not resist its beauty. Thus, the sacred legacy continues, enshrined in the hearts of the faithful, echoing through the corridors of time, and contributing to the divine symphony orchestrated by the Eternal Will Himself.

Methods Of Evangelization

The propagation of the Divine Will Movement and the dissemination of the teachings contained within the sacred pages of the Book of Heaven demands a multifaceted approach, tailored to capture the hearts and minds of the faithful. The goal of these efforts is not merely to inform but to inspire a profound transformation, drawing the faithful closer to the heart of God. Various methods of evangelization have proven efficacious, each imbued with the spirit of the Divine Will, enabling the faithful to grasp, cherish, and live according to these divine revelations.

First and foremost among these methods is the spoken word, delivered with fervent zeal through sermons, lectures, and personal testimonies. In the tradition of the early Christian Church, when the apostles spread the Good News through fervent preaching, so too must today's evangelists and preachers articulate the profundity of Luisa Piccarreta's revelations with clarity and passion. They must craft sermons that resonate with both the intellect and the soul, elucidating the divine mysteries and making them accessible to all.

The written word also stands as a pillar of evangelization. Just as the Holy Scriptures have been passed down through the ages, the dissemination of written materials such as books, pamphlets, and articles about the Divine Will serves to educate and inspire the faithful. These writings provide a lasting resource for personal study and reflection, allowing individuals to revisit the teachings and deepen their understanding over time. Modern technology amplifies this method, offering digital platforms where e-books and online articles can be accessed by a global audience.

Moreover, the formation of small study groups and prayer circles contributes significantly to the spread of these teachings. Gathering in intimate settings, believers can delve deeply into the writings of Luisa Piccarreta, discuss their insights, and share their spiritual experiences. Such communal endeavors not only foster intellectual comprehension but also nurture spiritual growth. These groups, through their collective devotion and shared learning, become microcosms of the larger Church, embodying the unity and fellowship of believers.

Incorporating the arts can also play a vital role in evangelization. Sacred music, dramatizations of Luisa's life, and visual arts inspired by the Divine Will Movement have the power to touch hearts in ways that transcend mere words. Artistic expressions can convey the beauty and profundity of the Divine Will, drawing individuals into a deeper appreciation and love for these sacred teachings. Concerts, plays, and exhibitions thus become venues of evangelization, reaching diverse audiences and igniting a yearning for the divine.

Personal witness remains an irreplaceable method of evangelization. The lives of those profoundly transformed by the Divine Will serve as living testaments to its power and truth. Sharing personal stories of conversion, healing, and spiritual renewal can move others to seek a similar transformation. Such testimonies, whether shared in person, through social media, or other mass communication channels, provide compelling evidence of the efficacy and fruits of living according to the Divine Will.

Educational institutions, from parish catechism classes to seminaries, must also be harnessed to effectively pass on these teachings. Curricula that include the writings of Luisa Piccarreta, alongside traditional theological and scriptural studies, ensure that future generations of clergy and lay leaders are well-versed in the Divine Will. Workshops, retreats, and conferences focused on these teachings can provide intensive learning experiences, thereby equipping participants with the knowledge and tools needed to evangelize effectively.

On a broader scale, the establishment of dedicated centers and missions focuses exclusively on promoting the Divine Will Movement. Such institutions can serve as resource hubs, offering extensive libraries, counseling, spiritual direction, and regular instructional programs. They become beacons of light, drawing the faithful and the curious alike, offering a place where the teachings are not only learned but lived in community.

Utilizing modern technology and media cannot be overlooked in our age. Websites, podcasts, video channels, and social media platforms provide unprecedented opportunities to reach vast audiences. Through these channels, detailed teachings, inspirational messages, and interactive discussions can be shared widely and instantaneously. The creation of engaging content that resonates with contemporary culture while remaining true to the core messages of the Divine Will is essential in this digital evangelization effort.

Furthermore, fostering relationships with clergy, theologians, and religious educators is critical for broadening the reach and acceptance of the Divine Will teachings. Providing them with comprehensive resources and supportive networks ensures that they are well-prepared to address the questions and concerns of their congregations. This collaboration strengthens the credibility and integration of the Divine Will Movement within the broader ecclesial community.

To measure the effectiveness of these evangelization methods, continuous feedback and assessment are necessary. Surveys, testimonials, and attendance records can provide valuable insights into what approaches resonate most with the faithful. This data-driven approach allows for the refinement and adaptation of evangelization strategies, ensuring that they remain dynamic and impactful.

Finally, let us not forget the power of prayer in our evangelization efforts. Just as Luisa Piccarreta's life was marked by profound prayer and contemplation, so too must our efforts be undergirded by supplication and intercession. Praying for the guidance of the Holy Spirit, for the hearts of the faithful to be opened, and for the strength to carry out this mission is paramount. Only through divine assistance can the true fruits of evangelization be realized.

In conclusion, the methods of evangelization for the Divine Will Movement are manifold and must be employed with great devotion and strategic intent. By embracing a variety of approaches, from spoken and written word to communal activities, artistic endeavors, personal testimonies, educational initiatives, technological advancements, and fervent prayer, we can ensure that these divine teachings reach and transform the hearts of many. Through our collective efforts, we honor the divine revelations granted to Luisa Piccarreta and fulfill our sacred duty to pass on the teachings for the awakening and edification of souls.

Resources For Education

In our noble mission to illuminate the hearts of faithful adherents, the edifying tapestry of the Divine Will Movement, the revered "Book of Heaven," and the teachings of Luisa Piccarreta demand a wellspring of scholarly and spiritual resources. Such were the resources designed, cultivated, and refined with divine inspiration to aid the studious minds of our Roman Catholic brethren. Verily, these resources serve not merely as tools for comprehension but as vessels of divine grace, steering souls towards the ineffable light.

The first bastion of knowledge comprises educational texts and manuscripts, meticulously penned by zealous scholars and holy theologians. They unravel the intricate tenets of the Divine Will, drawing from Luisa Piccarreta's volumes and aligning them with Sacred Tradition. These tomes offer exegesis that is both profound and accessible, delineating complex theological concepts with clarity akin to silver-beaming moonlight expelling nocturnal shadows.

Of paramount importance are the seminars and symposiums, convened within sanctified church halls and esteemed academic sanctuaries. These gatherings, graced by clergy and lay experts alike, offer an invaluable forum for discussing revelations contained within the Book of Heaven. Through robust dialogue and scholarly discourse, attendees are not merely witnesses but participants in a living pedagogical tradition, inspired by the Holy Spirit. Herein, minds are sharpened, and hearts are inflamed with divine fervor, echoing the vibrant oral tradition of early Christianity.

Modernity affords us the boons of technology, and so too we must harness it for the propagation of the Divine Will. Digital platforms become sacred spaces wherein souls yet yearning for knowledge might satiate their spiritual thirst. Websites, online forums, and video lectures provide a veritable cornucopia of information, discussion, and reflection on Luisa Piccarreta's divine revelations. With the blessed ubiquity of the internet, these resources bridge geographical chasms, uniting the faithful in an ever-expanding global ecclesia.

Additionally, multimedia presentations bring to life the sacred words captured in the Book of Heaven. Films, documentaries, and audio recordings narrate the life of Luisa and explore the intricacies of the Divine Will in a manner both engaging and elevating. The visual and auditory stimulation imparted by these forms ignites imagination and fosters a deeper, more visceral connection with the teachings, making ancient wisdom resonate with contemporary hearts.

No less essential are the catechetical materials tailored for different age groups within our congregations. From illustrated storybooks for the young aspirants to comprehensive guides for adult learners, these materials ensure that the divine narrative of the Divine Will can be grasped and cherished by all. Sunday schools, youth groups, and adult catechesis programs become the fertile grounds where such seeds of spiritual knowledge are sown and nurtured till they bloom into full understanding and devotion.

Peer study groups and prayer circles serve as sanctuaries of communion and collective inquiry. Here, the faithful gather to read, reflect, and pray upon the teachings preserved in the Book of Heaven. The fellowship and shared quest for divine truth within these assemblies mirror the apostolic gatherings of yore. Such group endeavors enlighten individual understanding through collective mystic experience, akin to light refracting through a prism, creating a dazzling spectrum of spiritual insight.

Integral to these efforts are the pastoral letters and encyclicals issued by our guiding shepherds—the bishops and priests—who draw upon their authority and wisdom to elucidate on the Divine Will's revelations. These ecclesiastical writings not only edify the masses but confer an apostolic endorsement that underpins the theological constructs drawn from Luisa Piccarreta's revelations, fostering unity and orthodoxy across the faithful assembly.

Lastly, pilgrimages to the sacred sites connected to Luisa Piccarreta offer an unparalleled spiritual education. Standing upon the very soil that witnessed her divine dialogues, the pilgrims are ensconced in an atmosphere thick with sanctity and historical resonance. Such physical journeys often precipitate inner transformations, creating indelible impressions upon the soul, deepening one's understanding and commitment to living within the Divine Will.

In sum, the veritable library of resources available to us today stands as a testimony to the providence and meticulous orchestration of our Divine Creator. These sources—whether tangible manuscripts or virtual lectures, communal gatherings, or solitary studies—serve a singular aim: to disseminate the wisdom contained within the Book of Heaven and to consecrate us ever closer to the Divine Will. May our endeavors in education continually reflect the spiraling heights of heavenly grace, leading the faithful ever upwards, from understanding into epiphany, from knowledge into transcendent union with the holy Divine Will.

Chapter 25: Future Of The Divine Will Movement

In the grandeur yet unfolding, the Divine Will Movement stands on the precipice of a future resplendent with divine promise and celestial fulfillment, as the seeds of Luisa Piccarreta's revelations find fertile soil in the hearts of the faithful. This movement, a heavenly orchestration, shall continue its sacred mission, calling forth a renewed vigor in living the Divine Will, as souls envisage an era where Heaven's peace mirrors our earthly pilgrimage. Propelled by an unyielding devotion to God's ineffable will, adherents will transform destinies, forging sanctity in the commonplace and bearing witness to a tapestry of divine love woven through daily acts. The task ahead is not solely in preserving the sacred texts but also in fostering an ardent communion that transcends temporal bounds, ensuring the Eternal Breath of God's Will permeates every facet of life. Thus, with unwavering fidelity and fervent embrace of this celestial mandate, the Eternal Kingdom shall flourish among men as foretold, beckoning a future radiant with divine splendor and unity, unfathomable to mere mortal comprehension.

Potential Developments

The Divine Will Movement, propelled by the heavenly insights bestowed upon Luisa Piccarreta and chronicled within the "Book of Heaven," stands at an epoch where its influence and reach could burgeon into unprecedented realms. Through the lenses of faith and spirituality, one can discern a myriad of avenues through which this celestial doctrine might further encapsulate the hearts and minds of the faithful, drawing them into deeper communion with the Divine Will.

Firstly, the movement may see a profound amplification in public and ecclesiastical recognition. As theologians and scholars delve more extensively into Piccarreta's volumes, their theological underpinnings may secure greater veneration within academic and religious institutions. Convincing interpretations that align seamlessly with magisterial teachings could herald a broader acceptance, especially as discussions around the Divine Will enrich doctrinal discourses. There is a veritable anticipation that the Church, in its wisdom, might cast an embracing light upon these nascent revelations, thereby encouraging scrutiny and acceptance by more clerical authorities.

Moreover, the potential canonization of Luisa Piccarreta, whose life remains an exemplar of heroic virtue, could catalyze an enormous upsurge in the movement's growth. This divine stamp of approval would offer indubitable credibility and inspire countless faithful to immerse themselves in her teachings. Consequently, the sanctity of her message may spark a renaissance in spiritual literature, birthing new commentaries, scholarly critiques, and hagiographies dedicated to unraveling the deeper mysteries of the Divine Will.

The laity could become even more fervent in their devotion, perhaps forming communal circles akin to the early Christian communities. Small groups dedicated to studying the "Book of Heaven" and practicing the life of the Divine Will might proliferate. These domestic churches would foster environments where believers can support one another in their divine journeys, fostering a shared sense of purpose and divine intimacy. Such fertile grounds of faith may indeed bear plentiful fruit, as neighborhoods and parishes are revitalized and unified under the celestial purpose.

Technological advancements may also play a pivotal role in propagating the Divine Will teachings. The advent of digital platforms and social media could act as conduits through which the writings of Luisa Piccarreta are disseminated to a global audience instantaneously. A surge in virtual seminars, webinars, and online communities could make it possible for isolated believers to partake in communal spiritual growth. Leverage of visual and audio mediums might transform the abstruse text into more accessible formats, thus ensuring the message resonates with a broader demographic.

Younger generations, particularly those in search of substantial spiritual encounters, may find the profundities of living in the Divine Will to be compelling. The call for a radical shift in lifestyle, predicated upon surrender and unity with God's will, presents an alternative to the secular and often ephemeral pleasures that currently dominate cultural paradigms. Educational institutions bearing Catholic heritage, recognizing this thirst for spiritual depth, could integrate these teachings within their curricula, guiding students towards both intellectual and spiritual enlightenment.

In addition, the translated editions of the "Book of Heaven" into various languages may enable the Divine Will Movement to cross sociocultural boundaries, reaching the faithful in lands afar and diverse. As translations emerge, non-English speaking communities can partake in the divine revelations, thereby fostering a universal brotherhood united under the celestial banners of God's Divine Will.

Furthermore, new forms of devotional practices rooted in the Divine Will could emerge, cultivating an enriched liturgical life. Enhanced forms of prayer, meditations, and Eucharistic adoration inspired by Piccarreta's writings might find their place within both private and communal worship settings. Devotees might develop novenas, feast days, and other spiritual exercises that align with the Divine Will teachings, thus integrating the movement's essence more profoundly into daily Catholic devotional life.

Institutional establishments such as retreat centers and seminaries might also embrace the Divine Will teachings more robustly. The formation of clergy and lay leaders knowledgeable in these spiritualities could further equip the Church to shepherd the faithful. This could catalyze the establishment of centers dedicated expressly to studying, teaching, and living out the Divine Will, where spiritual seekers can retreat for immersive experiences of divine union.

Thence, the movement may also gain traction through concrete acts of mercy and charity emanating from an alignment with the Divine Will. Inspired by divine guidance, hospitals, orphanages, and community outreach programs may arise, where the Gospel is lived out in tangible, transformative ways. This living embodiment of divine teachings could inspire a wave of compassionate service and justice that extends far beyond the bounds of the ecclesiastical confines into the broader realms of societal impact.

Despite these grand potentials, it is paramount to remain vigilant against misconceptions and misrepresentations of the Divine Will teachings. A cornerstone to future developments hinges upon authentic exegesis and dissemination of Piccarreta's writings. Ensuring faithful adherence to Church teachings whilst exploring these rich spiritual landscapes demands robust theological oversight and commitment. Only through a balanced and faithful exploration can the Divine Will Movement realize its divine potential, harmonizing with the broader tapestry of Catholic spirituality.

In summation, the future of the Divine Will Movement gleams with boundless possibilities. From ecclesiastical recognition, technological evangelism, and enriched communal devotions, the avenues for growth and impact are manifold. As the Church continues its divine journey, embracing and nurturing these heavenly revelations, the faithful may indeed grow to resemble more closely the divine image, living as vessels of the Eternal Will on earth.

Continuing The Mission

In the intricate tapestry woven by the Divine Will Movement, each thread represents a beacon of hope, a harbinger of divine grace, and an unwavering testament to the Heavenly Father's infinite love. As we stand on the precipice of furthering this sacred mission, we must shoulder the responsibility entrusted to us with fervor and unwavering conviction. The longevity and perseverance of this mission rest upon our shoulders, and its potential developments are contingent upon our alignment with divine guidance and communal unity.

The mission's impetus is not confined to ecclesiastical institutions; it extends into the hearts of every believer. To continue the Divine Will mission, we must cultivate an interior life that reflects the nobility of our commitment. Each act of love, every prayer whispered, and every kindness extended must conform to the Divine Will. As torchbearers of this celestial cause, our lives ought to exemplify the teachings by Luisa Piccarreta—serving as living treatises of heavenly doctrines.

The task before us involves disseminating these sacred teachings to a world increasingly mired in secular pursuits. Technology, social media, and modern communication platforms offer unprecedented avenues to broadcast the celestial melodies of the Divine Will Movement. Through podcasts, videos, and online forums, we can reach the ends of the earth, echoing the divine proclamations found in the Book of Heaven. Our mission should embrace these advancements with wisdom and discernment to penetrate the hearts of the global audience.

Evangelizing the message of the Divine Will requires not only strong faith but also scholarly acumen. Theological insights gained from the volumes of the Book of Heaven should be integrated into catechetical programs, homilies, and religious education curriculums. Collaborating with theologians, clergy, and educators, we can ensure that the profound wisdom imparted to Luisa Piccarreta is preserved, understood, and implemented with orthodoxy and fidelity to the sacred tradition of the Church.

One essential aspect of continuing this mission lies in fostering communal solidarity. Communities centered around the Divine Will must become sanctuaries of spiritual communion and mutual support. Collaborations with parish groups, prayer circles, and lay movements can create a robust network of faithful who embody and propagate the teachings. By sharing testimonies and experiences of living in the Divine Will, we reinforce our collective resolve and inspire others to embark on this sacred journey.

Moreover, we must engage in intercessory prayer and sacramental life to draw divine grace for this mission. Regular participation in the Holy Eucharist, Adoration, and the Sacrament of Reconciliation aligns our souls with divine decrees and bolsters our mission's spiritual strength. The integration of these sacraments into daily practice fortifies our spiritual armor, enabling us to withstand the spiritual battles intrinsic to such a lofty enterprise.

Engaging with youth is paramount for the perpetuation of the Divine Will Movement. By introducing young minds to the beauty and depth of these teachings, we plant seeds that will blossom into future generations of devoted followers. Youth ministries, retreats, and faith-based camps can serve as fertile grounds for nurturing young souls, imparting to them the knowledge and reverence required to sustain this sacred mission.

Additionally, we mustn't overlook the importance of responding adeptly to critiques and misconceptions. Through well-articulated defenses based on theological grounds, we can address objections and elucidate misunderstandings. Forming alliances with supportive clergy and scholars can aid in this endeavor, ensuring that our responses are both erudite and in harmony with Church doctrine. By affirming the Divine Will's congruence with sacred tradition, we eliminate doubts and invite skeptics into the fold.

Implementing the Divine Will teachings in daily life calls for practical steps that translate doctrine into action. Simple acts of charity, moments of silent prayer, and a sincere effort to live in perpetual communion with God's will transform abstract concepts into palpable realities. Every gesture imbued with divine intent becomes a testimony to the efficacy of Luisa's revelations, thus encouraging others to adopt these practices.

To maintain clarity and continuity, it is essential to safeguard the authenticity of the Divine Will's message. Avoiding dilution or distortion requires vigilance and fidelity to the original texts. Authorized translations, approved commentaries, and guided study groups ensure that the teachings remain unadulterated, empowering followers with genuine knowledge and insight into the divine mysteries.

Ultimately, the future of the Divine Will Movement hinges on our collective ability to embody these divine teachings and radiate their transformative power within our communities. The divine mandate calls for unwavering courage, intellectual rigor, and steadfast devotion to ensure that the mission continues uninhibited by temporal challenges. Through our dedicated efforts, we honor not only Luisa Piccarreta but also the divine source of her revelations, bringing us closer to the fullness of living in the Divine Will.

In summation, the mission's continuance calls for a harmonious blend of spiritual fervor, intellectual pursuit, and communal solidarity. We are the stewards of this divine legacy, charged with the sacred duty of preserving, practicing, and perpetuating the teachings imparted through the Book of Heaven. United in our cause, let us move forward, guided by the Divine Will, towards a future resplendent with heavenly grace and eternal wisdom.

Conclusion

As we draw this profound narrative to its sacred conclusion, let us contemplate the divine orchestration that has woven the Book of Heaven and the Divine Will Movement into the very fabric of our spiritual existence. In an era beset with secular distractions, the revelation imparted through Luisa Piccarreta constitutes a celestial beacon, guiding us towards a deeper union with the Holy Will of God. It is not mere happenstance but divine providence that has brought this magnum opus into our hands, to be cherished, scrutinized, and disseminated.

Immersing oneself in the teachings of the Book of Heaven is akin to navigating a celestial river of grace, where each page is a sacred ripple, propelling us towards the eternal ocean of God's Divine Will. The epic journey begins with understanding God's Plan and swiftly traverses through the luminously chronicled revelations bestowed upon Luisa. Her pious journey, marked by obedience and sanctity, illuminates the path for all souls yearning for divine intimacy. In this tapestry of divine revelation, the threads of sacred tradition and scripture are interwoven, affirming the sanctity and orthodoxy of the messages contained therein.

The volumes of the Book of Heaven do not merely narrate; they resonate with profound theological truths and spiritual urgency. Each volume, intricately summarized in the preceding chapters, unveils layers of divine wisdom, urging the soul towards complete abdication of self-will and full immersion in God's Will. The essence of the Divine Will transcends mere compliance;

it is a symbiotic union where human will becomes a willing partner in the eternal designs of the Divine.

As we proceed, it becomes paramount to acknowledge that the teachings of Luisa Piccarreta are not isolated spiritual musings but are steeped in and aligned with the sacred traditions of the Church. Through a meticulous examination, we find that the messages maintain a steadfast adherence to the scriptural and doctrinal foundations that have been the beacons of our faith through millennia. The Church, in her wisdom, has provided both an embrace of these revelations and prudent discernment, ensuring that the faithful may navigate these divine mysteries without peril of heretical deviation.

The spiritual fruits borne of the Divine Will Movement are manifold and bounteous. Through personal testimonies and transformative encounters, believers have experienced a profound renewal of faith, hope, and charity. The Movement has become a fertile ground where virtues are cultivated, and the Holy Spirit manifests His vivifying power. These real-world applications and testimonies provide empirical affirmations of the divine authenticity and the efficacy of Luisa's revelations.

Critics may arise, casting shadows of doubt over works of such divine profundity. Yet, it is through scholarly analysis, theological reflections, and the profound lived experiences of countless believers that the veracity and the divine origin of the Book of Heaven stand fortified against scepticism. Misunderstandings are inevitably clarified, and the Church's enduring wisdom prevails, fostering an environment of truth and reverent acceptance.

In living the Divine Will, we find ourselves partaking in a celestial symphony where every action, thought, and word harmonizes with God's eternal song. This calls for a commitment not just to understanding but to embodying the teachings in daily life. Practical steps and success stories animate the pages of this work, offering a blueprint for how to embed these divine teachings into the tapestry of our everyday existence, thus sanctifying the mundane and elevating the ordinary to the realm of the sacred.

Looking forward, the Divine Will Movement carries the torch of divine revelation into the future, lighting the path for generations yet unborn. Potential developments and the continuing mission invite us to partake in a spiritual renaissance, ensuring that the divine messages of the Book of Heaven are not relegated to the annals of history but are living, breathing realities shaping the future of the Church and all humanity.

In the twilight of this sacred examination, it is incumbent upon us to recognize that the Book of Heaven is not merely a compilation of divine messages; it is an invitation to a transformative way of living, a deeper immersion into the heart of God's Will. Embracing these teachings is not confined to intellectual assent but is a call to a radical transformation of one's life, aligning every heartbeat with the divine pulse of God's eternal love.

The journey we have undertaken through this book is but a prelude, an invitation to delve deeper into the boundless ocean of God's Will. As we stand on the precipice of such divine mysteries, may we move forward with hearts inflamed with love, minds illumined by truth, and souls committed to the sacred mission Lusia Piccarreta has left us.

Let us, therefore, go forth in the spirit of faith, hope, and charity, bearing witness to the transformative power of the Divine Will, and in doing so, fulfill our heavenly mandate. The consummation of this sacred narrative is not an end but a blessed beginning, a clarion call to all souls to embrace the Divine Will and, through it, to attain the divine intimacy for which we were created. In unity with God's eternal design, we shall find our ultimate fulfillment, our sanctification, and our eternal beatitude.

Appendix A: Appendix

Herein lies a collection of invaluable resources, a compendium of sacred texts, and guiding instruments dedicated to furthering one's journey into the profound depths of the Divine Will. This appendix offers an array of additional materials tailored to bolster your understanding and devotion. A meticulously curated assortment of prayers, meditations, and instructional guides await; each selected to enrich the spiritual tapestry woven throughout the Book of Heaven. Indeed, this final section stands as a beacon for the devout, a reservoir wherein seekers might find the spiritual sustenance necessary to imbibe fully the teachings and revelations granted unto Luisa Piccarreta, illuminating their path towards eternal communion with the Divine Will.

Additional Resources

In modernity's vast repository of spiritual texts, the Book of Heaven stands uniquely enthroned, a beacon of Divine illumination that beckons the faithful to plunge deeper into the mysteries of God's Will. Herein, to support your journey through this celestial narrative, we enumerate a collection of additional resources that shall aid your academic and devotional pursuits.

First and foremost, the primary text to immerse oneself in is the Book of Heaven itself. Authored by the mystic Luisa Piccarreta, this monumental work spans thirty-six volumes, each replete with revelations and divine communications. One must not only read but contemplate and pray over these texts to uncover the profound layers of spiritual wisdom enshrined within.

To bolster your comprehension, several study guides and commentaries by esteemed theologians are available. These works often include annotations, thematic explorations, and contextual background that provide clarity and depth to Luisa's mystical writings. Notables among these are the commentaries by Fr. Joseph Iannuzzi and the insights offered by the Association "Luisa Piccarreta – PFDV", which stands for Pious Association "Piccoli Figli della Divina Volontà", or Little Children of the Divine Will.

Equally important are the homilies and sermons of the Church Fathers, whose theological expositions often align or resonate with the teachings found in the Book of Heaven. Their ancient wisdom offers grounding, ensuring that interpretations remain in harmony with Sacred Tradition. St. Thomas Aquinas' Summa Theologica, and the writings of St. Augustine and St. John of the Cross, provide invaluable parallels and enrich the understanding of Divine Will.

Partake of the seminars and retreats organized by various associations devoted to the Divine Will Movement. These gatherings provide immersive experiences, foster communal prayer, and offer direct engagement with scholars who elucidate complex doctrines. Participating in such retreats can be pivotal in deepening one's personal conversion and understanding of living in the Divine Will.

The Diocesan resources include declarations, guidance, and pastoral letters from Bishops who oversee and shepherd the faithful in the correct understanding and application of Luisa's revelations. Peruse documents like the Vatican's Congregation for the Doctrine of the Faith's pronouncements on private revelations, which lend official ecclesiastical support and discernment.

One must also engage with scholarly analyses published in theological journals. These articles dissect the Latin and theological nuances, providing rigorous academic critiques and affirmations of Luisa's writings. Journals such as Nova et Vetera or Theological Studies often carry pieces by leading theologians who offer fresh perspectives and critical insights.

Devotional books and prayer aids designed specifically for those committed to the Divine Will Movement can be of great assistance. These texts often include prayers dictated by Jesus to Luisa, novenas, and meditative practices tailored to help the faithful live according to Divine Will daily. Key volumes include The Hours of the Passion and The Virgin Mary in the Kingdom of the Divine Will.

Personal testimonies, found in memoirs and biographical accounts, are also beneficial. These narratives recount the transformative experiences of individuals who have embraced the Divine Will, providing encouragement and a testament to the movement's efficacy. Texts like Biography of the Servant of God Luisa Piccarreta composed by various devotees, offer intimate glimpses into the life and sanctity of Luisa, thus inspiring the reader.

In the digital realm, websites and online forums offer an ever-accessible trove of materials. Scholarly websites dedicated to Luisa's works, such as luisapiccarretaofficial.org and divinewilltallahassee.com, serve as repositories of articles, manuscripts, and audio-visual materials. They provide invaluable resources for both solitary study and communal discussion.

Audio-visual resources such as lecture series, podcasts, and video documentaries also support the learner's journey. Platforms like YouTube or Vimeo feature lectures from respected theologians and clergy, offering detailed expositions on the teachings of the Divine Will. Moreover, podcasts aimed at daily reflection and living in Divine Will can seamlessly integrate into daily routines, fostering continual spiritual growth.

For those who seek a deeper academic engagement, enrolling in courses at theological seminaries or institutions dedicated to Marian studies and mysticism can be profoundly enriching. Institutions such as the Marian Library/International Marian Research Institute at the University of Dayton offer courses that cover mysticism and private revelations, providing a structured and scholarly approach to understanding Luisa's writings.

Community engagement through local Divine Will groups and associations is equally crucial. These groups offer a sense of belonging and shared purpose, allowing for discussion, prayer, and collective study. The collective wisdom generated in these group settings can often lead to greater insights and practical applications of the teachings.

In conclusion, as you traverse the luminous path drawn by the Book of Heaven, these additional resources shall serve as your steadfast companions. From commentaries to digital forums, and homilies to devotional retreats, each offering aids in uniting your soul more profoundly with the Divine Will. Let these resources illuminate your path, fostering a more profound, rich, and transformative spiritual journey.

Glossary Of Key Terms

To aid the faithful in comprehending the profound richness within "The Book of Heaven," this glossary shall serve as a beacon, illuminating the essence and mysteries contained therein.

- Divine Will – The supreme and paternal will of God, which governs all creation. It is described as the present and eternal fiat commanding the order and harmony throughout the cosmos.
- Book of Heaven – The opus of volumes penned by Luisa Piccarreta, revealing and elucidating the Divine Will. It is a treasure trove of divine revelations and celestial truths bestowed upon humanity.
- Eternal Fiat – The divine utterance by which God wills a thing into existence. This reverent command was first proclaimed in the creation of the universe and perpetuates in the governance of all existence.
- Fiat Voluntas Tua – Translated as "Thy Will Be Done," this petition encapsulates the prayer to live entirely within God's Will, mirroring the obedience of Christ and Mary.
- Divine Mercy – The boundless and infinite compassion of God towards humanity, characterized by forgiveness, love, and the desire to bring all into the fold of His Will.
- Divine Providence – God's intervention in the universe. It sustains and guides creation towards its ultimate end, ensuring that His Will is fulfilled in all occurrences, big or small.
- Triune God – The Holy Trinity, comprising the Father, the Son, and the Holy Spirit. It is a central tenet of Christian belief, signifying the unity of three distinct persons in one divine nature.
- Gift of Living in the Divine Will – A spiritual grace bestowed upon souls who surrender entirely to God's Will. It signifies a profound union with the divine, wherein one's life is harmonized with God's eternal desires.
- Luisa Piccarreta – The servant of God and humble writer through whom the Divine Will was vividly revealed. She is the devoted soul chosen to articulate the celestial messages contained in "The Book of Heaven."
- Sanctification – The process of becoming holy and conformed to the divine likeness. Through living in the Divine Will, souls aspire to achieve this state of sanctity.
- Acts in the Divine Will – The offerings, prayers, and deeds performed by a soul united with God's Will. These acts possess profound efficacy, contributing to divine harmony and salvation.
- Fusion with the Divine Will – The mystical state where the human will becomes one with the Divine Will, resulting in a sublime partnership with God's intentions and actions.

- Celestial Court – The assembly of angels and saints in heaven. Together, they worship God and intercede for humanity, embodying the Church triumphant in perpetual adoration of the Divine Will.
- Redemption – The deliverance from sin and its consequences brought about by the sacrifice of Jesus Christ. This foundational Christian doctrine finds new depth within the revelations of the Divine Will.
- Original Sin – The first act of disobedience by Adam and Eve, causing a rupture with the Divine Will. The journey of living in the Divine Will seeks to restore this primordial communion with God.
- Volition – The capacity and act of making choices or decisions. In the context of the Divine Will, it refers to aligning one's own desires with the supreme volition of God.
- Eucharistic Communion – The sacred reception of the Body and Blood of Christ in the sacrament of the Eucharist. It symbolizes a profound unity with Christ and fortifies the soul's resolve to live in the Divine Will.

May this glossary serve as a faithful guide on your journey through the sacred mysteries unfolded within "The Book of Heaven." Each term is a portal to deeper understanding and a step towards living fully in accordance with the Divine Will.